American Mathematics Competitions (AMC 10)
Preparation

Practice Tests

http://www.mymathcounts.com/index.php

This book can be used by students who are preparing for math competitions such as Mathcounts, American Mathematics Competition 10/12, and ARML (American Regions Mathematics League) Competition.

We field tested the problems in this book with students in our 2015 Mathcounts State Competition Training Groups. We would like to thank them for the valuable suggestions and corrections.

We tried our best to avoid any mistakes and typos. If you see any mistakes or typos, please contact mymathcounts@gmail.com so we can make improvements to the book.

Contributors

Yongcheng Chen, Ph.D., Author.
Guiling Chen, Owner, mymathcounts.com, Typesetter, Editor

ISBN-13: 978-1530036691
ISBN-10: 1530036690

Table of Contents

This page is intentionally left blank.

American Mathematics Competitions

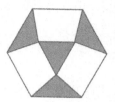

Practice 1
AMC 10

(American Mathematics Contest 10)

INSTRUCTIONS

1. This is a twenty-five question multiple choice test. Each question is followed by answers marked A, B, C, D and E. Only one of these is correct.

2. You will have 75 minutes to complete the test.

3. No aids are permitted other than scratch paper, graph paper, rulers, and erasers. No problems on the test will require the use of a calculator.

4. Figures are not necessarily drawn to scale.

5. SCORING: You will receive 6 points for each correct answer, 1.5 points for each problem left unanswered, and 0 points for each incorrect answer.

6. Do not guess the answer.

1. Let M, I, and T be distinct positive integers such that the product $M \times I \times T = 2015$. What is the largest possible value of the sum $M + I + T$?

(A) 8   (B) 44   (C) 155   (D) 403   (E) 409

2. $\dfrac{(2+1)(2^2+1)(2^4+1)(2^8+1)(2^{16}+1)(2^{32}+1)}{2^{64}-1} =$

(A) 2^{33} (B) 2^{64} (C) 1024   (D) 2   (E) 1

3. Each day, Jenny ate 30% of the jellybeans that were in her jar at the beginning of that day. At the end of second day, 98 remained. How many jellybeans were in the jar originally?

(A) 100   (B) 150   (C) 200   (D) 250   (E) 3005

4. Catherine pays an on-line service provider a fixed monthly fee plus an hourly charge for connect time. Her March bill was \$64.48, but in April her bill was \$51.54 because she used half as much connect time as in March. What is the fixed monthly fee?

(A) \$47.54   (B) \$46.06   (C) \$43.24   (D) \$40.42   (E) \$38.60

5. The lengths of three sides of a triangle are all integers. The perimeter of the triangle is an odd number and the difference of the lengths of two sides is 11. The possible length of the third side is:

(A) 13   (B) 12   (C) 11   (D) 10   (E) 9

6. The Fibonacci sequence $1, 1, 2, 3, 5, 8, 13, 21, \ldots$ starts with two 1's, and each term afterwards is the sum of its two predecessors. How many odd numbers are there in the first 2015 terms in the Fibonacci sequence?

(A) 1344   (B) 1342   (C) 1024   (D) 1007   (E) 1006

7. In rectangle $ABCD$, $BE : EC = 5 : 2$, $DF : CF = 2 : 1$. Find the area of triangle AEF if the area of the rectangle $ABCD$ is 1764.

(A) 134   (B) 342   (C) 462   (D) 707   (E) 764

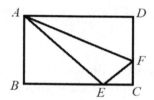

8. At Hope High School, 3/7 of the freshmen and 6/7 of the sophomores took the AMC 10. Given that the number of freshmen contestants is twice as many as the number of sophomore contestants, which of the following must be true?

(A) There are four times as many sophomores as freshmen.
(B) There are twice as many sophomores as freshmen.
(C) There are as many freshmen as sophomores.
(D) There are twice as many freshmen as sophomores.
(E) There are four times as many freshmen as sophomores.

9. Suppose that $|x - \pi| = 2q$, where $x < \pi$. What is the value of $x + 3q$?

(A) π (B) 3   (C) $\pi - 2q$ (D) $\pi + q$ (E) $\pi + 5q$

10. The length and width of a rectangle are positive integers. The perimeter and the area have the same numerical values. What is the sum of all possible values of the area of the rectangle?

(A) 16   (B) 18   (C) 24   (D) 34   (E) 46

11. Two different prime numbers between 12 and 32 are chosen. When their sum is subtracted from their product, which of the following numbers could be obtained?

(A) 159   (B) 210   (C) 359   (D) 802   (E) 1079

12. At each stage, a new square is drawn on each side of the perimeter of the figure in the previous stage. Figures show four stages of 1, 5, 13, and 25 nonoverlapping unit squares, respectively. If the pattern were continued, how many unit squares will be in Stage 200?

A) 79601   (B) 78804   (C) 49402   (D) 40199   (E) 39402

Stage 1   Stage 2   Stage 3   Stage 4

13. How many ways can five people line up behind four registers?

(A) 6720   (B) 120   (C) 720   (D) 394   (E) 6240

14. Mr. Wang gave an exam in a mathematics class of five students. He entered the scores in random order into a spreadsheet, which recalculated the class average after each score was entered. Mr. Wang noticed that after each score was entered, the average was always an integer. The scores (listed in ascending order) were 74, 77, 88, 94, and 97. What was the last score Mr. Wang entered?

(A) 77   (B) 88   (C) 74   (D) 94   (E) 97

15. What is the value of $\dfrac{a-b}{a+b}$ if $a^2 + b^2 = 4ab$, where $a < b < 0$.

(A) $\sqrt{3}$ (B) $-\dfrac{\sqrt{3}}{3}$ (C) $\dfrac{\sqrt{3}}{3}$ (D) $-\sqrt{3}$ (E) 1

16. The horizontally and vertically adjacent points in this square grid are 1 cm apart. Segment AB meets segment CD at E. Find the length of segment BE.

(A) $\dfrac{2\sqrt{5}}{3}$ (B) $\dfrac{4\sqrt{5}}{3}$ (C) $\dfrac{2\sqrt{3}}{5}$

(D) $\dfrac{5\sqrt{2}}{3}$ (E) $\dfrac{\sqrt{5}}{3}$

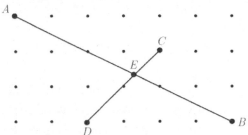

17. Betsy has an incredible coin machine. When she puts in a quarter, it returns five nickels; when he puts in a nickel, it returns five pennies; and when she puts in a penny, it returns nine quarters. Betsy starts with just one quarter. Which of the following amounts could she have after using the machine many times?

(A) $7.73   (B) $7.27   (C) $7.16   (D) $7.05   (E) $6.97

18. Charles walks completely around the boundary of a square. From any point on his path he can see exactly 2 km horizontally in all directions. The area of the region consisting of all points Charles can see is $144 + 4\pi$ during his walk. What is the length of the side of the square?

(A) 4   (B) 6   (C) 8   (D) 10   (E) 12

19. In square units, what is the largest possible area a rectangle inscribed in the triangle shown here can have? $BC = 100$ cm. $AH = 80$ cm.

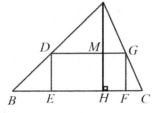

(A) 2000   (B) 6000   (C) 5000   (D) 4000   (E) 1200

20. Let a, b, and c be distinct real numbers. Find $a : b : c$ if a, b, and c form an arithmetic sequence and b, a, and c form a geometric sequence.

(A) 2 : 1 : 4   (B) (− 2) : 1 : 4   (C) 2 : (− 2) : 4   (D) 2 : 1 : (− 2)   (E) 3 : 1 : 4

21. Alex, Bob, and Charlie are students who participate in three different clubs (Math, Science, and Writing) with each person in only one club. They are from three schools: Hope School, Cox School, and Ashley School, not necessarily in that order. Alex is not from Hope School, Bob is not from Cox School. The student from Hope School is not in the Science club, the student from Cox School is in the Math club. Bob is not in the Writing club. Which school is Charlie from and what club is he in?

(A) Hope School and Writing club.   (B) Cox School and Math club.
(C) Ashley and Science club.   (D) Hope School and Science club.
(E) Cox School and Science club.

22. One morning Alex and Bob took a math contest. Alex got a ninth of the total number of problems on the contest wrong and Bob got seven problems correct. The number of the problems answered correctly by both people is one sixth of the total number of problems on the contest. How many problem were answered correctly by Alex?

(A) 32   (B) 22   (C) 12   (D) 8   (E) 7

23. When the mean, median, and mode of the list 11, 3, 6, 3, 5, 3, x are arranged in increasing order, they form a non-constant arithmetic progression. What is the sum of all possible real value of x ?

(A) 4   (B) 25   (C) 39   (D) 43   (E) 54

24. What is the sum of all values of z for which $f(5z) = 21$ and f is a function defined by $f(\frac{x}{5}) = x^2 + x + 1$.

(A) $-\dfrac{1}{13}$ (B) $-\dfrac{1}{25}$ (C) -5 (D) $\dfrac{5}{7}$ (E) 5

25. In year N, the 200th day of the year is a Sunday. In year $N + 1$, the 100th day is also a Sunday. On what day of the week did the 300th day of year $N - 1$ occur?

(A) Thursday (B) Friday   (C) Saturday (D) Sunday   (E) Monday

ANSWER KEYS

1. E.
2. E.
3. C.
4. E.
5. B.
6. A.
7. C.
8. E.
9. D.
10. D.
11. C.
12. A.
13. A.
14. C.
15. C.
16. B.
17. E.
18. D.
19. A.
20. B.
21. A.
22. A.
23. E.
24. B.
25. E.

SOLUTIONS

1. E.

Factor 2015 into primes to get $2015 = 5 \times 13 \times 31$. The largest possible sum of three distinct factors whose product is the one which combines the two largest prime factors, namely $M = 13 \times 31 = 403$, $I = 5$, and $T = 1$, so the largest possible sum is $403 + 5 + 1 = 409$.

2. E.

$$(2+1)(2^2+1)(2^4+1)(2^8+1)(2^{16}+1)(2^{32}+1)$$
$$= (2-1)(2+1)(2^2+1)(2^4+1)(2^8+1)(2^{16}+1)(2^{32}+1)$$
$$= (2^2-1)(2^2+1)(2^4+1)(2^8+1)(2^{16}+1)(2^{32}+1)$$
$$= (2^4-1)(2^4+1)(2^8+1)(2^{16}+1)(2^{32}+1)$$
$$= (2^8-1)(2^8+1)(2^{16}+1)(2^{32}+1)$$
$$= (2^{16}-1)(2^{16}+1)(2^{32}+1) = (2^{32}-1)(2^{32}+1) = 2^{64}-1$$

So the answer is $\dfrac{2^{64}-1}{2^{64}-1} = 1$.

3. C.

Since Jenny ate 30% of the jellybeans remaining each day, 70% of the jellybeans are left at the end of each day. If x is the number of jellybeans in the jar originally, then $(0.7)^2 x = 98$. Thus $x = 200$.

4. E.

Method 1:

Since Catherine paid $\$64.48 - \$51.54 = \$12.94$ less in April, her March connect time must have cost her $\$12.94 \times 2 = \$25.98$. Therefore, her monthly fee is $\$64.48 - \$25.98 = \$38.60$.

Method 2:

Let m be the fixed monthly fee and t be the connect time fee.

$m + t = 64.48$ (1)

$m + \dfrac{t}{2} = 51.54$ (2)

$(2) \times 2 - (1)$: $m = 38.60$.

5. B.

Let a, b, and c be the lengths of the sides of the triangle. Let $a - b = 11$. So one of a and b is even and another one is odd. We know that $a + b + c$ is odd. Thus c must be even. By triangle inequality, $c > a - b = 11$. The possible length is then 12.

6. A.

We see the pattern:

1, 1, 2,

3, 5, 8,

13, 21, 34,

55, 89, 144,

…………..

There are two odd numbers every three terms.

$2015 = 671 \times 3 + 2$.

We get $671 \times 2 + 2 = 1344$ odd numbers.

7. C.

Method 1:

Let the areas of triangles AEF, ADF, ABE, EFC, be $S_{\triangle AEF}$, $S_{\triangle ADF}$, $S_{\triangle EFC}$, $S_{\triangle AEF}$, respectively.

Since $DF : CF = 2 : 1$, $S_{\triangle ADF} = \dfrac{1}{3} S_{ABCD} = \dfrac{1764}{3} = 588$

Since $BE : EC = 5 : 2$, $S_{\triangle ABE} = \dfrac{1}{2} \times \dfrac{5}{7} S_{ABCD} = \dfrac{5 \times 1764}{14} = 630$.

$$S_{\triangle EFC} = \frac{1}{2} \times \frac{2}{7} \times \frac{1}{3} S_{ABCD} = \frac{1764}{21} = 84.$$

Therefore $S_{\triangle AEF} = 1764 - 588 - 630 - 84 = 462$

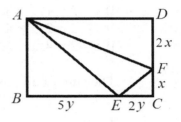

Method 2:

Let $BE = 5y$ and $DF = 2x$.

The area of the rectangle $ABCD$ is $1764 = (5y + 2y)(2x + x) = 21xy$

Thus $xy = 1764 / 21 = 84$.

The following relationship is true: $S_{ABCD} = 2S_{\triangle AEF} + BE \times DF$

$\Rightarrow 1764 = 2S_{\triangle AEF} + 5y \times 2x \quad \Rightarrow \quad 1764 = 2S_{\triangle AEF} + 10 \times 84$

$\Rightarrow S_{\triangle AEF} = \dfrac{1764 - 840}{2} = 462$.

8. E.

Let f and s represent the numbers of freshmen and sophomores at the school, respectively.

According to the given condition, $\dfrac{3}{7} f = 2 \times \dfrac{6}{7} s \quad \Rightarrow f = 4s$.

That is, there are four times as many freshmen as sophomores.

9. D.

Since $x < \pi$, $|x - \pi| = \pi - x$. If $\pi - x = 2q$, then $x = \pi - 2q$. Thus $x + 3q = \pi + q$.

10. D.

Let x and y represent the length and width of the rectangle, with $x \geq y$, respectively.

$xy = 2(x + y)$.

Solving for y: $y = \dfrac{2x}{x-2} = \dfrac{2(x-2)+4}{x-2} = 2 + \dfrac{4}{x-2}$.

Since y is a positive integer, $x - 2$ must be a factor of 4.

If $x - 2 = 1$, $x = 3$. Then $y = 6$. We ignore this case since $x < y$.

If $x - 2 = 2$, $x = 4$. Then $y = 4$. The area is $4 \times 4 = 16$.

If $x - 2 = 4$, $x = 6$. Then $y = 3$. The area is $6 \times 3 = 18$.

The sum of all possible values of the area of the rectangle is $16 + 18 = 34$.

11. C.

There are six prime numbers between 12 and 32: 13, 17, 19, 23, 29, and 31. Let $m = xy - (x + y) = (x - 1)(y - 1) - 1$. So m must be odd.

The smallest possible value of m is $13 \cdot 17 - (13 + 17) = 191$ and the largest possible value is $29 \cdot 31 - (29 + 31) = 839$. The only possibility among the options is 359, and we see that $359 = 13 \cdot 31 - (13 + 31)$.

12. A.

$$a_{200} = \binom{200-1}{0} + 4\binom{200-1}{1} + 4\binom{200-1}{2}$$

$$= 1 + 4 \times 199 + 4 \times \frac{199 \times 198}{2} = 79601$$

So Stage 200 has 79601 unit squares.

13. A.

Method 1:

The four registers can have the following amount of people:

5	0	0	0	$\binom{5}{5} \times 5! \times \dfrac{4!}{3!} = 480$
4	1	0	0	$\binom{5}{4} \times 4! \times \dfrac{4!}{2!} = 1440$

3	2	0	0	$\binom{5}{3} \times 3! \times 2! \times \dfrac{4!}{2!} = 1440$
3	1	1	0	$\binom{5}{3} \times 3! \times \binom{2}{1} \times \binom{1}{1} \times \dfrac{4!}{2!} = 1440$
2	2	1	0	$\binom{5}{2} \times 2! \times \binom{3}{2} \times 2! \times \dfrac{4!}{2!} = 1440$
2	1	1	1	$\binom{5}{2} \times 2! \times \binom{3}{1} \times \binom{2}{1} \times \dfrac{4!}{3!} = 480$

The answer is $480 + 1440 \times 4 + 480 = 6720$.

Method 2: Line the three registers in a row:

1   2   3   4

Person A has 4 choices (register 1, register 2, register 3, or register 4).

Person B has 5 choices (suppose person A is standing in front of register 1, B can go to register 1, or register 2, or register 3, or register 4. If B goes to register 1, he has 2 choices: in front of A or behind A).

Similarly, C has 6 choices, D has 7 choices, and E has 8 choices.
The total number of ways is $4 \times 5 \times 6 \times 7 \times 8 = 6720$.

Method 3:
A general formula for these types of questions:
For m machines and n people, there are N ways to line up and

13

$$N = \binom{m+n-1}{n} \times n!.$$

In this case, $N = \binom{4+5-1}{5} \times 5! = \binom{8}{5} \times 5! = 6720$.

14. C.

The sum of the scores of the first n students must be a multiple of n. The two scores of the first two students must have the same parity. The sum of the scores of the first three students must be divisible by 3. The remainders when 77, 88, 74, 94, and 97 are divided by 3 are 2, 1, 2, 1, and 1, respectively. We see that the only sum of three scores divisible by 3 is $88 + 94 + 97 = 279$. So the first two scores entered are 88 and 94 (in some order), and the third score is 97. $279 + x$ must be a multiple of 4. So x must be an odd number. Thus we choose 77 from the two numbers: 77 and 74. $279 + 77 = 356 = 4 \times 89$. Then we know that the fourth score is 77 and the score is 74.

15. C.

Subtracting $2ab$ from both sides of the original equation:

$a^2 + b^2 - 2ab = 4ab - 2ab$ or $(a-b)^2 = 2ab$

Since $a < b < 0$, $a - b < 0$. $\Rightarrow$ $a - b = -\sqrt{2ab}$ (1)

Adding $2ab$ to both sides of the original equation: $a^2 + b^2 + 2ab = 4ab + 2ab$ or $(a+b)^2 = 6ab$.

Since $a < b < 0$, $a + b < 0$. So $a + b = -\sqrt{6ab}$ (2)

(1) ÷ (2): $\dfrac{a-b}{a+b} = \dfrac{-\sqrt{2ab}}{-\sqrt{6ab}} = \dfrac{\sqrt{3}}{3}$.

16. B.

Connect BD. Draw $CF \,/\!/\, BD$. $CF = 2$ and $BD = 4$. Applying Pythagorean

Theorem to triangle BDF: $FB = \sqrt{DF^2 + BD^2} = \sqrt{2^2 + 4^2} = 2\sqrt{5}$ or

$FE + BE = 2\sqrt{5}$ (1)

Triangle CFE is similar to triangle DBE. So

we have $\dfrac{FC}{BD} = \dfrac{FE}{BE} \Rightarrow \dfrac{2}{4} = \dfrac{FE}{BE}$

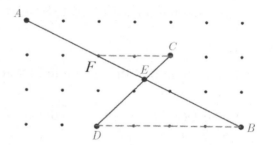

$\Rightarrow \qquad BE = 2FE$ (2)

Substituting (2) into (1): $\dfrac{BE}{2} + BE = 2\sqrt{5}$

$\Rightarrow \qquad \dfrac{3BE}{2} = 2\sqrt{5} \quad \Rightarrow \qquad BE = \dfrac{4\sqrt{5}}{3}.$

17. E.

Note that when Betsy puts a quarter or a nickel in the machine, the total values of the coins do not change. If she puts a penny in the machine, it returns 5 quarters. This increases the total value of Betsy's coins by \$2.24. Hence, Betsy must have \$0.25 + \$2.24n after n uses of the last exchange. Only option E is of this form: $697 = 25 + 224 \times 3$. In cents, option A is 101 more than a multiple of 224, B is 55 more than a multiple of 224, C is 44 more than a multiple of 224, and D is 33 more than a multiple of 224.

18. D.

Let x be the length of the side of the square.
At any point on Charles' walk, he can see all the points inside a circle of radius 2 km. The portion of the viewable region inside the square consists of the interior of the square except for a smaller square with side length $x - 4$ km. This portion of the viewable region has area $x^2 - (x-4)^2 = 8x - 16$ km^2. The portion of the viewable region outside the square

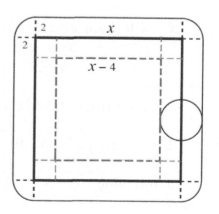

consists of four rectangles, each x km by 2 km, and four quarter-circles (which make one whole circle), each with a radius of 2 km. This portion of the viewable region has area $4 \times 2x + \pi \times 2^2 = (8x + 4\pi)$ km^2 . The area of the entire viewable region is $8x - 16 + (8x + 4\pi) = 144 + 4\pi \Rightarrow 16x - 160 = 0 \Rightarrow x = 10$.

19. A.

Let the length of the rectangle be x and the width be y.

Since $DG // BC$, $\triangle ADG \sim \triangle ABC$

$$\frac{DG}{BC} = \frac{AM}{AH} \quad \Rightarrow \quad \frac{x}{100} = \frac{80 - y}{80} \Rightarrow 4x = 5(80 - y) \Rightarrow x = 100 - \frac{5}{4}y.$$

Let the area of rectangle $DEFG$ be S.

$$S = xy = (100 - \frac{5}{4}y)y = -\frac{5}{4}y^2 + 100y = -\frac{5}{4}(y^2 - 80y) = -\frac{5}{4}(y - 40)^2 + 2000.$$

The greatest value is 2000 (when $x = 50$ and $y = 40$).

20. B.

Method 1:

Since a, b, and c form an arithmetic sequence, we have $2b = a + c$ (1)

Since b, a, and c form a geometric sequence, we have $a^2 = bc$ (2)

We will eliminate c from (1) and (2).

(1) $\times b$: $2b^2 = ab + bc$ (3)

(2) $-$ (3): $a^2 + ab - 2b^2 = 0 \Rightarrow \quad (a + 2b)(a - b) = 0$

We know that a, b, and c be distinct real numbers. So $(a - b) \ne 0$.

Then we have $a + 2b = 0$ $\Rightarrow$ $a = -2b$ $\Rightarrow$ $a : b = -2 : 1$

Substituting $a = -2b$ into (1): $c = 4b$ $\Rightarrow$ $b : c = 1 : 4$

The answer is $a : b : c = (-2) : 1 : 4$.

Method 2:
Since a, b, and c form an arithmetic sequence, we have $\quad 2b = a + c \quad$ (1)

Since b, a, and c form a geometric sequence, we have $\quad a^2 = bc \quad$ (2)

We will eliminate b from (1) and (2).
(2) $\times$ 2: $\quad 2a^2 = 2bc \quad\quad\quad\quad\quad\quad\quad\quad$ (3)

Substituting (1) into (3): $2a^2 = (a + c)c \Rightarrow 2a^2 - ac - c^2 = 0 \Rightarrow (2a + c)(a - c) = 0$

We know that a, b, and c be distinct real numbers. So $(a - c) \neq 0$.
Then we have $2a + c = 0 \quad\quad \Rightarrow \quad\quad -2a = c$

Substituting $\quad c = -2a$ into (1): $\quad 2b = a - 2a \quad \Rightarrow \quad 2b = -a \Rightarrow a : b = -2 : 1$
$c = 4b \Rightarrow \quad b : c = 1 : 4$.
The answer is $a : b : c = (-2) : 1 : 4$.

21. A.

We use dash line to indicate a no relationship and a solid line a yes relationship.
The figure below shows the information we are given.

From figure, we know that the student from hope School must be in writing club. The student from Ashley School must be in Science Club. Bob must be in

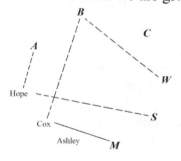
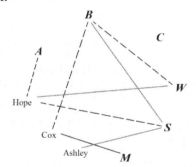

Science Club. Therefore Bob is from Ashley School. Since Alex is not from Hope

School, so he is from Cox School. Thus Charlie is from Hope School and is in Writing Club.

22. A.

As shown in the Venn diagram, n is the total number of problems in the test, c is the number of problems both got correct, a is the number of problems only Alex got correct, b is the number of problems only Bob got correct, and d is the number of problems both got wrong. Thus $b + d$ is the number of problems Alex got wrong.

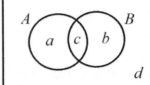

$c = n/6$
$c + b = 7$
$b + d = n/9$
$n - d = (a + c) + (b + c) - c \implies n = (a + c) + (b + c) - c + d = (a + c) + (b + d)$
$\implies (a + c) = n - (b + d) = n - n/9 = 8n/9.$

Since c is an integer, n must be a multiple of 6.

Since $b + d$ is an integer, n must be a multiple of 9. Thus n must be a multiple of 18 and $(a + c)$ must be a multiple of 18.

When n is 18, $c = 3$, $b = 4$, $d = -2$ (ignored).

When n is 36, $c = 6$, $b = 1$, $d = 3$ (worked).
$(a + c) = 8n/9 = 32.$

23. E.

If x were less than or equal to 3, then 3 would be both the median and the mode of the list. Thus $x > 3$. Consider the two cases $3 < x < 5$, and $x \geq 5$.

Case 1: If $3 < x < 5$, then 3 is the mode, x is the median, and $(31 + x)/7$ is the mean,
We have

$$\frac{x+3}{2} = \frac{31+x}{7} \Rightarrow \quad 2(31+x) = 7(x+3) \quad \Rightarrow \quad x = \frac{41}{5}$$

$$\frac{\frac{31+x}{7}+x}{2} = 3 \Rightarrow \quad \frac{31+8x}{7} = 6 \quad \Rightarrow \quad x = \frac{11}{8}$$

$$\frac{\frac{31+x}{7}+3}{2} = x \Rightarrow \quad \frac{31+x}{7}+3 = 2x \quad \Rightarrow \quad x = 4.$$

$x = 4$ is the only value between 3 and 5.

Case 2: If $x \geq 5$, then 5 is the median, 3 is the mode, and $(31 + x)/7$ is the mean. We have

$$\frac{5+3}{2} = \frac{31+x}{7} \Rightarrow \quad \frac{31+x}{7} = 4 \quad \Rightarrow \quad x = -3$$

$$\frac{\frac{31+x}{7}+5}{2} = 3 \Rightarrow \quad \frac{31+x}{7} = 6 \quad \Rightarrow \quad x = 11$$

$$\frac{\frac{31+x}{7}+3}{2} = 5 \Rightarrow \quad \frac{31+x}{7} = 10 \quad \Rightarrow \quad x = 39.$$

11 and 39 are the values greater than or equal to 5.
Thus the x-value sum to $4 + 11 + 39 = 54$.

24. B.
Method 1:
Let $25z = x$.

$$f(\frac{x}{5}) = x^2 + x + 1 \quad \Rightarrow \quad f(\frac{25z}{5}) = f(5z) = (25z)^2 + 25z + 1 = 21$$

Simplifying:
$$625z^2 + 25z - 20 = 0 \Rightarrow \quad 125z^2 + 5z - 4 = 0 \quad \Rightarrow \quad (25z - 4)(5z + 1) = 0.$$

Solving for z: $z = -\frac{1}{5}$ or $\frac{4}{25}$.

The sum of all values of z is $-\dfrac{1}{25}$.

Method 2:

Let $25z = x$.

$$f(\frac{x}{5}) = x^2 + x + 1 \quad \Rightarrow \quad f(\frac{25z}{5}) = f(5z) = (25z)^2 + 25z + 1 = 21$$

Simplifying:

$$625z^2 + 25z - 20 = 0 \quad \Rightarrow \quad 125z^2 + 5z - 4 = 0$$

By Vieta's formula, the sum of the roots is $-\dfrac{5}{125} = -\dfrac{1}{25}$.

25. E.

Method 1:

If N is not a leap year, the 100th day of year $N + 1$ is $365 - 200 + 100 = 265$ days after a Sunday, and thus is a Saturday, since $265 = 37 \times 7 + 6$. Thus, year $N + 1$ is a leap year because the 100th day of year $N + 1$ is Sunday (as given). It follows that year $N - 1$ is not a leap year. Therefore, the 300th day of year $N - 1$ precedes the given Sunday in year N by $365 - 200 + 165 = 330$ days ($330 = 7 \times 47 + 1$), and therefore is a Monday.

Method 2:

We need to know two things before we begin to solve the problem:

(1) There is one leap year every 4 years.

(2) For regular years, Monday in year N will be Tuesday in year $N + 1$. (Because $365 \equiv 1 \bmod 7$).

We are given that in year N,

$200 \equiv 4 \pmod 7$. The 200th day of the year is a Sunday.

Remainder	0	1	2	3	4	5	6
Day	W	Th	F	Sat	Sun	Mon	Tue

Also in year N,

$100 \equiv 2 \pmod 7$. The 100th day of the year is a Friday.

$300 \equiv 6$ (mod 7). The 300th day of the year is a Tuesday.

In year $N + 1$, the 100th day should be a Saturday, one day from Friday.

We are given that in year $N + 1$, the 100th day is a Sunday. Therefore, year $N + 1$ is a leap year and we can conclude that year $N - 1$ is not a leap year.

In year $N - 1$, the 300th day of the year will be one day before Tuesday, or Monday.

American Mathematics Competitions

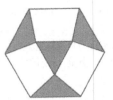

Practice 2
AMC 10

(American Mathematics Contest 10)

INSTRUCTIONS

1. This is a twenty-five question multiple choice test. Each question is followed by answers marked A, B, C, D and E. Only one of these is correct.

2. You will have 75 minutes to complete the test.

3. No aids are permitted other than scratch paper, graph paper, rulers, and erasers. No problems on the test will require the use of a calculator.

4. Figures are not necessarily drawn to scale.

5. SCORING: You will receive 6 points for each correct answer, 1.5 points for each problem left unanswered, and 0 points for each incorrect answer.

1. The median of the list $n, n + 2, n + 3, n + 5, n + 7, n + 8, n + 11, n + 14, n + 16, n + 19$ is 20. What is the mean?

(A) 14   (B) 16   (C) 17   (D) 20   (E) 21

2. A number x is 11 more than the product of its reciprocal and its additive inverse.
In which interval does the number lie?

(A) $-4 \leq x \leq -12$ (B) $-2 < x \leq 2$ (C) $0 < x \leq 11$
(D) $2 < x \leq 9$ (E) $4 < x \leq 6$

3. The sum of three numbers is S. Suppose 5 is added to each number and then each of the resulting numbers is tripled. What is the sum of the final three numbers?

(A) $3S$ (B) $3S + 5$ (C) $3S + 15$ (D) $3S + 40$ (E) $3S + 45$

4. What is the maximum number for the possible points of intersection of two concave quadrilaterals?

(A) 18   (B) 16   (C) 12   (D) 8   (E) 6

5. How many of the eleven nets of a cube pictured below have at least one line of symmetry?

(A) 2   (B) 7   (C) 6   (D) 5   (E) 3

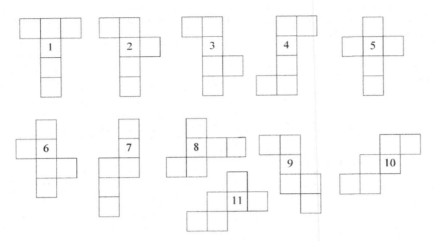

6. Let $S(n)$ denote the sum of the digits of the integer n. For example, $S(24) = 6$. Suppose N is a two-digit number such that $N = 3S(N) + 8$. What is the units digit of N?

(A) 2   (B) 3   (C) 7   (D) 8   (E) 9

7. When the decimal point of a certain positive decimal number is moved two places to the right, the new number is two times the sum of the original number and the reciprocal of the original number. What is the product of 21 and the original number?

(A) 1   (B) 2   (C) 3   (D) 4   (E) 5

8. Alex, Bob, Cathy, Danny, and Emma are tutors in the school math lab. Their schedule is as follows: Alex works every fifth school day, Bob works every eight school day, Cathy works every ninth school day, Danny works every twelfth school day, and Emma works every fifteenth school day. Today they are all working in the math lab. In how many school days from today will they next be together tutoring in the lab?

(A) 142   (B) 184   (C) 226   (D) 278   (E) 360

9. The state income tax where Kerry lives is levied at the rate of p % of the first $38000 of annual income plus $(p + 3)$% of any amount above $38000. Kerry noticed that the state income tax he paid amounted to $(p + 1.5)$% of his annual income. What was his annual income?

(A) $38000   (B) $42000   (C) $55,000   (D) $62,000   (E) $76,000

10. If x, y, and z are positive with $xy = 21$, $xz = 28$, and $yz = 12$, then $x^2 + y^2 + z^2$

(A) 28   (B) 39   (C) 50   (D) 62   (E) 74

11. Consider the rectangle as shown. The first figure is a rectangle cutting into four regions by its two diagonals. There are 6 line segments in figure (1), 12 line segments in figure (2), and 18 line segments in figure (3). If the pattern continues, how many line segments are in the 100th figure?

(A) 396   (B) 600   (C) 800   (D) 1,000   (E) 1,404

            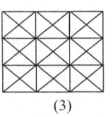

(1)   (2)   (3)

12. If n is the product of four consecutive integers and that n is divisible by 11. Which of the following is not necessarily a divisor of n?

(A) 66   (B) 44   (C) 24   (D) 22   (E) 18

13. When $\sqrt{5}$ is separated into an integer part and a decimal part, the decimal part can be written as m. Find $m^2 + 2(m + \sqrt{5})$.

(A) 4   (B) 5   (C) 6   (D) 7   (E) 8

14. Mr. Mathis' class had m boys and 11 girls. Mr. English's class had nine boys and n girls. Two classes raised the same amount of money during a charity sell, with each class raising $$(mn + 9m + 11n + 145)$. It was known that every student participated in the activity and each student donated the same amount of money (a whole dollar amount) more than $30. How much money was donated by each student?

(A) $78   (B) $68   (C) $57   (D) $47   (E) $34

15. A street has parallel curbs 60 feet apart. A crosswalk bounded by two parallel stripes crosses the street at an angle. The length of the curb between the stripes is 10 feet and each stripe is 75 feet long. Find the distance, in feet, between the stripes.

(A) 9   (B) 10   (C) 12   (D) 8   (E) 6

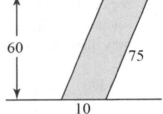

16. In a riddle contest, three points are awarded to answer a difficult riddle correctly and one point is awarded to answer an easy riddle correctly. It is known that 8 people get 1 point, seven people get 2 points, six people get 3 points, five people get 4 points, four people get 5 points, and three people get 6 points. How many people answered exactly two riddles correctly if each person can only answer at most four riddles?

(A) 16   (B) 8   (C) 14   (D) 12   (E) 15

17. What is the volume of the cones below that is formed from a 100.8° sector of a circle of radius 25?

(A) $\dfrac{1000\pi}{3}$ (B) 406π (C) 1000π (D) $\dfrac{500\pi}{3}$ (E) 392π

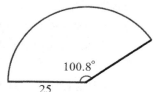

18. The plane is tiled by congruent squares and congruent pentagons as indicated. Find the ratio of the areas of shaded square to shaded octagon.

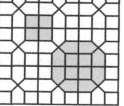

(A) $\dfrac{2}{7}$ (B) $\dfrac{4}{15}$ (C) $\dfrac{2}{5}$ (D) $\dfrac{1}{2}$ (E) $\dfrac{1}{3}$

19. Pam wants to buy seven donuts from an ample supply of five types of donuts: Chocolate Iced, White Iced, Maple Iced, Orange Iced, and Strawberry Iced. How many different selections are possible?

(A) 210   (B) 330   (C) 365   (D) 240   (E) 172

20. A regular octagon is formed by cutting an isosceles right triangle from each of the corners of a square with sides of length 2015. What is the area of the octagon?

(A) $2015^2(2\sqrt{2}-2)$ (B) $2015^2(4\sqrt{2}-5)$

(C) $2015^2(\sqrt{2}-5)$ (D) $2015^2(4\sqrt{2}-1)$ (E) $2015^2(\sqrt{2}-1)$

21. A right circular cylinder with its diameter equal to its height is inscribed in a right circular cone. The cone has diameter 16 and altitude 48, and the axes of the cylinder and cone coincide. Find the volume of the solid inside the cone but outside the cylinder.

(A) 1024π (B) 988π (C) 592π (D) 432π (E) 240π

22. In the magic square shown, the sums of the numbers in each row, column, and diagonal are the same. What number does the letter C represent?

(A) 3   (B) 8   (C) 9   (D) 10 (E) 12

C		6
		7
4		

23. A box contains exactly nine chips, five red and four white. Chips are randomly removed one at a time without replacement until all the red chips are drawn or all the white chips are drawn. What is the probability that the last chip drawn is red?

(A) $\dfrac{2}{3}$ (B) $\dfrac{4}{9}$ (C) $\dfrac{2}{5}$ (D) $\dfrac{5}{9}$ (E) $\dfrac{3}{4}$

24. In parallelogram $ABCD$, $AE \perp BC$, $AF \perp CD$. $\angle EAF = 45°$. $AE + AF = 2\sqrt{2}$. Find the perimeter of $ABCD$.

(A) $4\sqrt{2}$.   (B) $2(\sqrt{2}+2)$.   (C) $2(\sqrt{2}+1)$.
(D) 8.   (E) 4.

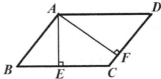

25. How many positive integers not exceeding 2015 are multiples of 5 or 13 but not 31?

(A) 448   (B) 510   (C) 509   (D) 449   (E) 511

ANSWER KEYS

1. E.
2. C.
3. E.
4. B.
5. A.
6. B.
7. C.
8. E.
9. E.
10. E.
11. B.
12. E.
13. B.
14. D.
15. D.
16. E.
17. E.
18. A.
19. B.
20. A.
21. C.
22. B.
23. B.
24. D.
25. B.

SOLUTIONS

1. E.

The middle number in the 10-number list is $[(n+7)+(n+8)]/2 = n + 15/2$, which is given as 20. Thus $n = 25/2$. The mean is $(10n + 85)/10 = 210/10 = 21$.

2. C.

The reciprocal of x is $1/x$, and the additive inverse of x is $-x$. The product of these is $\dfrac{1}{x} \times (-x) = -1$. So $x = -1 + 11 = 10$, which is in the interval $0 < x \le 11$.

3. E.

Suppose the two numbers are x, y, and z.
$x + y + z = S$
Then the desired sum is
$3(x + 5) + 3(y + 5) + 3(z + 5) = 3(x + y + z) + 45 = 3S + 45$.

4. B.

5. A.

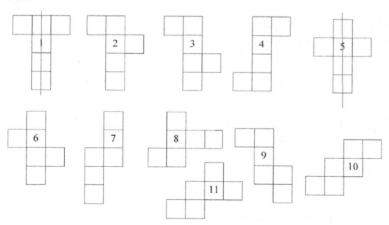

6. B.

Suppose $N = 10a + b$. Then $10a + b = 3(a + b) + 8 \quad \Rightarrow \quad 7a = 2(b + 4)$.

So a must be even and $b + 4$ is a multiple of 7. Since b is a digit less than 10, $b = 3$.

7. C.

If x is the number, then moving the decimal point two places to the right is the same as multiplying x by 100. That is, $100x = 2(x + \dfrac{1}{x})$ $\Rightarrow$ $50x = x + \dfrac{1}{x}$

$\Rightarrow$ $x^2 = \dfrac{1}{49}$. Since x is positive, it follows that $x = 1/7 = 0.\overline{142857}$.

The product and 21 and $0.\overline{142857}$ is 3.

8. E.

The number of school days until they will next be together is the least common multiple of 5, 8, 9, 12 and 15, which is 360.

9. E.

If Kristin's annual income is $x \geq 38,000$ dollars, then

$$\frac{p}{100} \times 38000 + \frac{p+3}{100} \times (x - 38000) = \frac{p+1.5}{100} \times x$$

Multiplying by 100 and expanding yields
$38,000p + px + 3x - 38,000p - 114,000 = px + 1.5x$.
So, $1.5x = 114,000$ and $x = 76,000$.

10. E.

Take the product of the equations to get $(xy)(xz)(yz) = 21 \times 28 \times 12 = 3^2 \times 4^2 \times 7^2$, or $xyz = 3 \times 4 \times 7$.

$$\frac{xyz}{xy} = \frac{3 \times 4 \times 7}{21} \qquad \Rightarrow z = 4.$$

Similarly, $x = 7$ and $y = 3$. $x^2 + y^2 + z^2 = 3^2 + 4^2 + 7^2 = 5^2 + 7^2 = 74$.

11. B.

The first figure has $6 + 0 \times 6$ line segments.
The second figure has $6 + 1 \times 6$ line segments.
The third figure has $6 + 2 \times 6$ line segments.
The nth figure has $6 + (n - 1) \times 6$ line segments.
The 100th figure has $6 + (100 - 1) \times 6 = 600$ line segments.

12. E.

We know that the product of k consecutive integers is divisible by $k!$. Therefore, the product of the four integers is divisible by 24. Since 11 is a divisor of the product, n is also divisible by 11. So n is divisible by any factor of $24 \times 11 = 2^3 \times 3 \times 11$.

However, 18 contains two factors of 3, and n does not. For example, $10 \times 11 \times 12 \times 13$ is divisible by 11, but not by 18.

13. B.

Since m is the decimal part of $\sqrt{5}$, $m = \sqrt{5} - 2 \Rightarrow m + 2 = \sqrt{5}$ (1)
$m^2 + 2(m + \sqrt{5}) =$
$m^2 + 2m + 2\sqrt{5} = m(m + 2) + 2\sqrt{5} = (\sqrt{5} - 2)(\sqrt{5}) + 2\sqrt{5} = 5 - 2\sqrt{5} + 2\sqrt{5} = 5$

14. D.

$mn + 9m + 11n + 145$ is divisible by both $m + 11$ and $n + 9$.
We have $mn + 9m + 11n + 145 = (m + 11)(n + 9) + 46$.
So 46 is divisible by both $m + 11$ and $n + 9$.
We know that $46 = 1 \times 46 = 2 \times 23$

Therefore we have
Case 1:
$n + 9 = 23$ $\Rightarrow$ $n = 14$ and $m = 12$
Each student donated $\dfrac{(m + 11)(n + 9) + 46}{m + 11} = \dfrac{(11 + 11)(14 + 9) + 46}{12 + 11} = 25$ (ignored since it is less than 30).

Case 2:

$n + 9 = 46$ $\Rightarrow$ $n = 37$ and $m = 35$

Each student donated $\dfrac{(m+11)(n+9)+46}{m+11} = \dfrac{(35+11)(37+9)+46}{35+11} = 47$.

So the answer is $47.

15. D.
Method 1:
The crosswalk is in the shape of a parallelogram with base 10 feet and altitude 60 feet, so its area is $10 \times 60 = 600$ ft^2. But viewed another way, the parallelogram has base 75 feet and altitude equal to the distance between the stripes, so this distance must be $600/75 = 8$ feet.
Method 2:
Draw $AB \perp CE$, and $CD \perp DE$. Triangles ABC is similar to triangle CDE.

$\dfrac{AB}{AC} = \dfrac{CD}{CE}$ $\Rightarrow$ $\dfrac{60}{75} = \dfrac{CD}{10}$ $\Rightarrow$ $CD = \dfrac{60 \times 10}{75} = 8$.

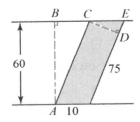

16. E.
People who answered exactly two riddles correct can two easy riddles, two hard riddles, or one easy and one hard riddle. So the possible points are: $1 + 1 = 2$ points, $1 + 3 = 4$ points, or $3 + 3 = 6$ points.

People who get 6 points may answer 6 easy riddles correctly. But we know that each person can only answer four questions at most, so people who get 6 points must answer two hard riddles correctly. Therefore the answer is $7 + 5 + 3 = 15$.

17. E.
The slant height of the cone is 25, the radius of the sector.
Let r be the radius of the cone.

$\dfrac{360}{2\pi \times 25} = \dfrac{100.8}{2\pi r}$ $\Rightarrow$ $r = 7$

Triangle ABC is a 7- 24 – 25 right triangle.

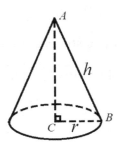

34

The volume of the cone is $V = \dfrac{1}{3} \times \pi \times 7^2 \times 24 = 392\pi$.

18. A.

The shaded squares consists of 4 smaller squares and the shaded octagon consists of 14 smaller squares.

The ratio is $\dfrac{4}{14} = \dfrac{2}{7}$

 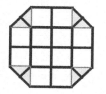 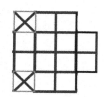

19. B.

The number of possible selections is the number of non-negative integer solutions of the equation $a + b + c + d + e = 7$.

The solution is $\dbinom{7+5-1}{5-1} = \dbinom{11}{4} = \dfrac{11 \times 10 \times 9 \times 8}{4 \times 3 \times 2 \times 1} = 330$

20. A.

Let x represent the length of each side of the octagon, which is also the length of the hypotenuse of each of the right triangles. Each leg of the right

triangles has length $\dfrac{\sqrt{2}}{2} x$.

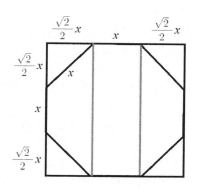

So $2 \times \dfrac{\sqrt{2}}{2} x + x = 2015 \Rightarrow x = \dfrac{2015}{\sqrt{2}+1} = 2015(\sqrt{2}-1)$.

The area of the octagon is $2015^2 - 4 \times \dfrac{\dfrac{\sqrt{2}}{2} x \times \dfrac{\sqrt{2}}{2} x}{2} = 2015^2 - x^2$

$= 2015^2 - [2015(\sqrt{2}-1)]^2 = 2015^2[1 - (\sqrt{2}-1)^2] = 2015^2(2\sqrt{2}-2)$.

21. C.

Let the cylinder have radius r and height $2r$. Since $\triangle APQ$ is similar to $\triangle AOB$, we

have $\dfrac{48}{8} = \dfrac{48 - 2r}{r} \Rightarrow 6 = \dfrac{48 - 2r}{r}$

$\Rightarrow 6r = 48 - 2r \Rightarrow r = \dfrac{48}{8} = 6$.

$V = \dfrac{1}{3}\pi \times 8^2 \times 48 - \pi \times 6^2 \times 12 = 592\pi$

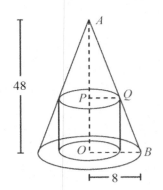
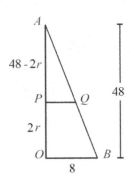

22. B.

We calculate a first as shown. $a = \dfrac{S}{3} = \dfrac{4 + 6 + a}{3}$, S is the magic sum.

$3a = 4 + 6 + a \Rightarrow a = 5$.
So $S = 3a = 15$ and $b = 15 - 7 - 6 = 2$ and $c = 15 - 5 - 2 = 8$.

c		6
	a	7
4		b

23. B.

Think of continuing the drawing until all nine chips are removed from the box.
One of the ordering is

$\boxed{R\ R\ R\ R\ R\ W\ W\ W\ W}$.

There are $\dfrac{9!}{5! \times 4!} = 126$ possible orderings of the colors in total.

Any orderings that end in W represent drawings that would have ended when the fifth red chip was drawn.

$\boxed{R\ R\ R\ R\ R\ W\ W\ W}\quad W$

There are $\dfrac{8!}{5! \times 3!} = 56$ orderings that end in W.

The answer is then $\dfrac{56}{126} = \dfrac{4}{9}$.

24. D.

In parallelogram $ABCD$, $AF \perp CD$.

Since $AB // CD$, $AF \perp AB$. We also know that $\angle EAF = 45°$, $\angle BAE = 45°$

In Rt$\triangle ABE$, $\angle BAE = 45°$. $AE = BE$, $AB = \sqrt{2}AE$.

Similarly, $AD = \sqrt{2}AF$. The perimeter is then $2(AB + AD) = 2\sqrt{2}\,(AE + AF) = 8$.

25. B.

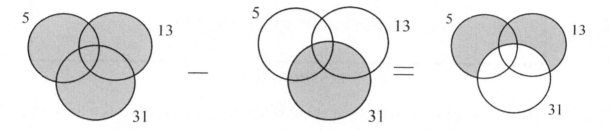

The number of positive integers not exceeding 2015 are multiples of 5 or 13 or 31 is

$$\left\lfloor \frac{2015}{5} \right\rfloor + \left\lfloor \frac{2015}{13} \right\rfloor + \left\lfloor \frac{2015}{31} \right\rfloor - \left\lfloor \frac{2015}{5 \times 13} \right\rfloor - \left\lfloor \frac{2015}{13 \times 31} \right\rfloor - \left\lfloor \frac{2015}{31 \times 5} \right\rfloor + \left\lfloor \frac{2015}{5 \times 13 \times 31} \right\rfloor$$
$$= 403 + 155 + 65 - 31 - 5 - 13 + 1 = 575.$$

The number of positive integers not exceeding 2015 that are multiples of 9 is
$$\left\lfloor \frac{2015}{31} \right\rfloor = 65.$$

The answer is $575 - 65 = 510$.

American Mathematics Competitions

Practice 3
AMC 10

(American Mathematics Contest 10)

INSTRUCTIONS

1. This is a twenty-five question multiple choice test. Each question is followed by answers marked A, B, C, D and E. Only one of these is correct.

2. You will have 75 minutes to complete the test.

3. No aids are permitted other than scratch paper, graph paper, rulers, and erasers. No problems on the test will require the use of a calculator.

4. Figures are not necessarily drawn to scale.

5. SCORING: You will receive 6 points for each correct answer, 1.5 points for each problem left unanswered, and 0 points for each incorrect answer.

1. Find the ratio $\dfrac{2015^{2016} - 2015^{2014}}{2015^{2015} - 2015^{2014}}$.

(A) 1   (B) 2013   (C) 2014   (D) 2015   (E) 2016

2. For the negative number a, simplify $\sqrt{a^2} + \sqrt{(1-a)^2}$.

(A) 1   (B) $1 - 2a$ (C) $2a - 1$ (D) $a - 1$ (E) -1

3. A list of numbers by a certain pattern is as follows: $-2015, -2011, -2007, -2003, \ldots$ The sum of the first n terms has the smallest value. Then n is

(A) 500   (B) 501   (C) 502   (D) 503   (E) 504

4. What is the value of $(5x - 3)(6x + 1) - (5x - 3)6x + 11$ when $x = 8$?

(A) 50   (B) 48   (C) 40   (D) 21   (E) 12

5. Circles of radius 5 and 7 are externally tangent and are circumscribed by a third circle, as shown in the figure. Find the area of the shaded region.

(A) 70π (B) 75π (C) 82π (D) 35π (E) 41π

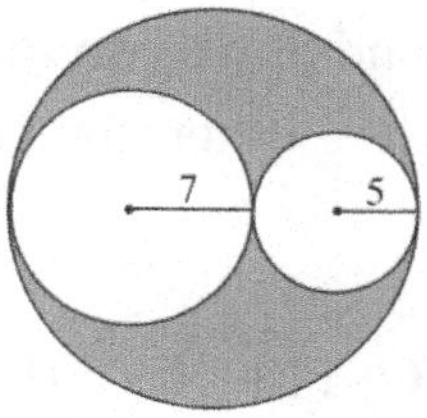

6. Cindy was asked by her teacher to subtract 5 from a certain number and then divide the result by 11. Instead, she subtracted 11 and then divided the result by 5, giving an answer of 111. What would her answer have been had she worked the problem correctly?

(A) 15   (B) 34   (C) 43   (D) 53   (E) 51

7. If an arc of $75°$ on circle A has the same length as an arc of $55°$ on circle B, then the ratio of the area of circle A to the area of circle B is

(A) $\dfrac{11}{15}$ (B) $\dfrac{11}{25}$ (C) $\dfrac{121}{225}$ (D) $\dfrac{2}{5}$ (E) $\dfrac{12}{25}$

8. Suppose July of year N has five Saturdays. Which of the following must occur five times in August of year N ?

(A) Tuesday (B) Wednesday (C) Thursday (D) Friday   (E) Sunday

9. Suppose x, y, and z are three numbers for which $2015z - 2014x = 2016$ and $2015y + 4029x = 4029$. The average of the three numbers x, y, and z is

(A) 1 (B) 3   (C) 6   (D) 9   (E) not uniquely determined

10. Using the digits 1, 2, 3, 4, and 5, we can form 120 five-digit numbers. If these numbers are arranged in increasing order, then the number 54123 occupies position

(A) 112   (B) 113   (C) 114   (D) 115   (E) 116

11. James wants to move 64 tons of goods from one store to another store. He has two types of pickup trucks: one can carry 7 tons and one can carry 4 tons. The larger truck will consume 14 gallon of gas and the smaller truck will consume 9 gallons of gas for one trip. What is the smallest number of gallons of gas he needs to finish the job?

(A) 120   (B) 130   (C) 142   (D) 150   (E) 160

12. Mr. Ernie Bird leaves his house for work at exactly 9:00 A.M. every morning. When he decreases his speed by 8 miles per hour, he arrives at his workplace five minutes late. When he increases his speed by 12 miles per hour, he arrives five minutes early. At what average speed, in miles per hour, should Mr. Bird drive to arrive at his workplace precisely on time? The distance from his home to work is 12 miles.

(A) 45   (B) 48   (C) 50   (D) 55   (E) 58

13. As shown in the figure, $\angle B = 90°$, $AB = 3$, $BC = 4$, $CD = 13$, $AD = 12$. Find the area of quadrilateral $ABCD$.

(A) 32   (B) 34   (C) 36   (D) 38   (E) 45

14. Both roots of the quadratic equation $x^2 - 73x + k = 0$ are prime numbers. Find the value of k.

(A) 73   (B) 146   (C) 142   (D) 144   (E) 150

15. How many ways are there to write 26 as the sum of two or more prime numbers?

(A) 2   (B) 3   (C) 4   (D) 5   (E) 6

16. For how many integers n is $\dfrac{n}{40-n}$ the square of an integer?

(A) 1   (B) 2   (C) 3   (D) 4   (E) 10

17. As shown in the figure, E is a point on the side AD and F is a point on the side BC of rectangle $ABCD$. Connect AF, DF, BE, and CE. AF meets BE at P. CE meets DF at Q. Find the shaded area if the area of triangle ABP is 25 cm^2 and the area of triangle CDQ is 35 cm^2.

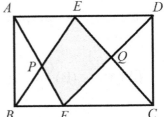

(A) 25   (B) 35   (C) 45   (D) 55   (E) 60.

18. A 4 × 4 × 4 wooden cube is painted on all 6 faces and then cut into 64 unit cubes. One unit cube is randomly selected and rolled. What is the probability that exactly one of the five visible faces is painted?

(A) 5/16   (B) 7/16   (C) 15/31   (D) 31/64   (E) 1/2

19. Barker's doghouse has a regular pentagonal base that measures one yard on each side.   He is tethered to a vertex with a two-yard rope. What is the area, in square yards, of the region outside the doghouse that Spot can reach?

(A) $\dfrac{46\pi}{15}$ (B) 3π (C) $\dfrac{13\pi}{5}$ (D) $\dfrac{47\pi}{15}$ (E) $\dfrac{16\pi}{5}$

20. Four congruent triangular corners are cut off a 23×37 rectangle. The resulting octagon has eight edges of equal length. What is this length?

(A) 13   (B) 14   (C) 15   (D) 16   (E) 17

21. Seven girls (Abby, Betty, Cathy, Debra, Emma, Fern, and Gabby) travel with one boy (Harry) to a math contest. They have five hotel rooms, numbered 1 through 5. Each room can hold up to two people, and the boy has to have a room to himself. How many different ways are there to assign the students to the rooms?

(A) 10,000   (B) 12,000   (C) 12,600   (D) 13,000   (E) 13,200

22. Both a and b are rational numbers. Find $a^2b + ab^2$ if
$2a^2 - 2ab + b^2 + 6a + 9 = 0.$

(A) 27   (B) -27 (C) 54   (D) -54 (E) 20

23. As shown in the figure, the area of triangle ABC is 36. Find $S_{\triangle ADE}$, the area of triangle ADE if $S_{\triangle BDE} = S_{\triangle DEC} = S_{\triangle AEC}$

(A) 5 (B) 6   (C) 7   (D) 9   (E) 12

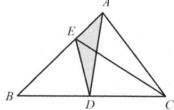

24. Tina randomly selects two distinct numbers from the set $\{1, 2, 3, 4, 5, 6\}$, and Sergio randomly selects a number from the set $\{1, 2, \ldots, 10, 11\}$. The probability that Sergio's number is smaller than the sum of the two numbers chosen by Tina is

(A) $\dfrac{6}{11}$ 　　　 (B) $\dfrac{53}{99}$ 　　　 (C) $\dfrac{1}{2}$ 　　　 (D) $\dfrac{10}{11}$ 　　　 (E) $\dfrac{5}{11}$

25. In trapezoid $ABCD$ with bases AB and CD, the total shaded area is 40 cm^2. The area of triangle AOB is 5 cm^2. The area of trapezoid $ABCD$ is

(A) 185 　　 (B) 195 　　 (C) 165 　　 (D) 125 　　 (E) 160

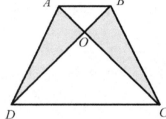

ANSWER KEYS

1. E.
2. B.
3. E.
4. B.
5. A.
6. E.
7. C.
8. A.
9. A.
10. D.
11. B.
12. B.
13. C.
14. C.
15. E.
16. D.
17. E.
18. B.
19. E.
20. A.
21. C.
22. D.
23. B.
24. A.
25. D.

SOLUTIONS:

1. E.
$$\frac{2015^{2016} - 2015^{2014}}{2015^{2015} - 2015^{2014}} = \frac{2015^{2014}(2015^2 - 1)}{2015^{2014}(2015 - 1)} = \frac{2015^2 - 1}{2015 - 1} = \frac{(2015 - 1)(2015 + 1)}{2015 - 1}$$
$$= 2015 + 1 = 2016.$$

2. B.
$$\sqrt{a^2} + \sqrt{(1-a)^2} = -a + (1-a) = 1 - 2a$$

3. E.
The list show an arithmetic sequence with the first term $- 2015$ and common difference 4.
The general term is $a_n = -2015 + (n-1) \times 4 = 4n - 2019$.
Since we want the smallest sum, we let $a_n \leq 0$. So we have $4n - 2019 \leq 0$
$$\Rightarrow 4n \leq 2019$$
$$\Rightarrow n \leq \frac{2019}{4} = 504\frac{3}{4}.$$ So we know that $a_{504} \leq 0$, and $a_{505} > 0$.
Thus the sum of the first 504 terms has the smallest value.

4. B.
$(5x - 3)(6x + 1) - (5x - 3)6x + 11$
$= (5x - 3)(6x + 1 - 6x) + 11 = 5x - 3 + 11 = 5x + 8$

When $x = 8$, we have the value $5 \times 8 + 8 = 48$.

5. A.
The diameter of the large circle is $7 \times 2 + 5 \times 2 = 24$, so its radius is 12. Hence, the area of the shaded region is
$\pi(12^2) - \pi(7^2) - \pi(5^2) = \pi(144 - 49 - 25) = 70\pi.$

6. E.

Let x be the number she was given. Her calculations produce

$$\frac{x-11}{5} = 111 \quad \Rightarrow \quad x-11 = 555 \Rightarrow x = 566.$$

The correct answer is $\dfrac{566-5}{11} = 51$.

7. C.

Let R_A be the radius of circle A, let $R_B = 2\pi R_B$ be the radius of circle B, and let L the common length of the two arcs. Then

$$\frac{75}{360} \times 2\pi \times R_A = \frac{55}{360} \times 2\pi \times R_B = L$$

Therefore $\dfrac{R_A}{R_B} = \dfrac{55}{75} = \dfrac{11}{15}$. So the ratio of the areas is $(\dfrac{R_A}{R_B})^2 = (\dfrac{11}{15})^2 = \dfrac{121}{225}$

8. A.

Since July has 31 days, the last Saturday of five Saturdays must be one of the last three days of July.

If the last Saturday is July 31, we get five Sundays, Mondays, and Tuesdays in August.

Saturday	**Sunday**	**Monday**	**Tuesday**	Wednesday	Thursday	Friday
7/31	8/1	8/2	8/3	8/4	8/5	8/6
8/7	8/8	8/9	8/10			
8/14	8/2	8/3	8/17			
8/21	8/2	8/3	8/24			
8/28	8/29	8/30	8/31			

Similarly, if the last Saturday is July 30, we get five Mondays, Tuesdays, and Wednesdays in August.

If the last Saturday is July 29, we get five Tuesdays, Wednesdays, and Thursdays in August.

Therefore, Tuesday must occur five times in August.

9. A.

Adding 1001 $2015z - 2014x = 2016$ and

$2015y + 4029x = 4029$ yields $2015x + 2015y + 2015z = 6045$.

$x + y + z = 3 \implies (x + y + z)/3 = 1$.

10. D.

The last number, which occupies position 120, is 54321. Immediately preceding this we have 54312, 54231, 54213, 54132, and 54123. The position of the word 54123 is consequently 115.

11. B.

We see that $\dfrac{7}{4} > \dfrac{14}{9}$. So he needs to use the larger truck more times in order to save gas.

$64 = 7 \times 9 + 1$. He can use larger truck 9 times and smaller truck one time, which will consume $9 \times 14 + 9 = 135$ gallons of gas.

$64 = 7 \times 8 + 4 + 4$. He can also use larger truck 8 times and smaller truck two times, which will consume $8 \times 14 + 9 + 9 = = 130$ gallons of gas.

The answer is 130.

12. B.

Let x be the desired average speed.

$$\frac{d}{x-8} - \frac{5}{60} = \frac{d}{x+12} + \frac{5}{60} \implies \frac{12}{x-8} - \frac{12}{x+12} = \frac{5}{60} + \frac{5}{60} \implies$$

$$\frac{1}{x-8} - \frac{1}{x+12} = \frac{1}{120} \implies \frac{x+12-(x-8)}{(x-8)(x+12)} = \frac{1}{120} \implies$$

$$\frac{20}{(x-8)(x+12)} = \frac{1}{120} \implies x^2 + 4x - 2496 = 0$$

$$(x-48)(x+52) = 0 \implies x = 48 .$$

13. C.

$\triangle ACD$ is a right triangle and $\angle DAC=90°$.

Area of $ABCD$ = Area of $\triangle ABC$ + Area of $\triangle ACD$

$\dfrac{1}{2} \times 3 \times 4 + \dfrac{1}{2} \times 12 \times 5 = 6 + 30 = 36$ square units.

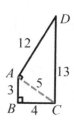

14. C.

Let p and q be two primes that are roots of $x^2 - 73x + k = 0$.

By Vieta's Theorem, we have $p + q = 73$, and $p \times q = k$.

Since 73 is odd, one of the primes must be 2 and the other 71. Thus, there is exactly one possible value for k, namely $k = p \times q = 2 \times 71 = 142$.

15. E.

The prime numbers useful are 2, 3, 5, 7, 11, 13, 17, 19, and 23. We know that 26 is even. So we have the following cases.

Case 1: odd + odd.
$26 = 3 + 23 = 7 + 19$.

Case 2: even + odd + odd.
$26 = 2 + 5 + 19 = 2 + 7 + 17 = 2 + 11 + 13$

Case 3: odd + odd + odd + odd
$26 = 3 + 5 + 7 + 11$.
We get 6 ways.

16. D.

If $\dfrac{n}{40-n} = m^2$, for some integer $m \geq 0$, then

$n = \dfrac{40m^2}{m^2+1} = \dfrac{40m^2+40-40}{m^2+1} = 40 - \dfrac{40}{m^2+1}$.

Since n is an integer, $m^2 + 1$ must be a factor of $40 = 2^3 \times 5$.

$m^2 + 1 = 1 \quad \Rightarrow \quad m = 0 \quad \Rightarrow \quad n = 0$ and $\dfrac{n}{40-n} = 0$.

$m^2 + 1 = 2 \quad \Rightarrow \quad m = 1$ or $m = -1 \quad \Rightarrow \quad n = 20$ and $\dfrac{n}{40-n} = 1$.

$m^2 + 1 = 4 \quad$ (no integer solution).

$m^2 + 1 = 5 \quad \Rightarrow \quad m = 2$ or $m = -2 \quad \Rightarrow \quad n = 32$ and $\dfrac{n}{40-n} = 4$.

$m^2 + 1 = 8 \quad$ (no integer solution).

$m^2 + 1 = 10 \quad \Rightarrow \quad m = 3$ or $m = -3 \quad \Rightarrow \quad n = 36$ and $\dfrac{n}{40-n} = 1$.

$m^2 + 1 = 20 \quad$ (no integer solution).
$m^2 + 1 = 40 \quad$ (no integer solution).
The values of n are 0, 20, 32, and 36.

17. E.

Let the shaded area be x.

We now that $S_{\Delta BEC} = \dfrac{1}{2} S_{ABCD}$, and

$$S_{\Delta ABF} + S_{\Delta CDF} = \frac{AB \times BF}{2} + \frac{CD \times FC}{2} = \frac{AB(BF + FC)}{2} = \frac{AB \times BC}{2} = \frac{1}{2} S_{ABCD}.$$

Thus $S_{\Delta BEC} = S_{\Delta ABF} + S_{\Delta CDF}$ or

We see that $S_{\Delta BEC} = S_{\Delta BPF} + S_{\Delta QFC} + x$ and

$S_{\Delta ABF} + S_{\Delta CDF} = S_{\Delta ABP} + S_{\Delta BPF} + S_{\Delta CDQ} + S_{\Delta QFC}$.

So $S_{\Delta BPF} + S_{\Delta QFC} + x =$

$S_{\Delta ABP} + S_{\Delta BPF} + S_{\Delta CDQ} + S_{\Delta QFC} \Rightarrow x = S_{\Delta ABP} + S_{\Delta CDQ} = 25 + 35 = 60$.

18. B.

There are $6 \times 4 = 24$ cubes with one face painted, and these show one painted face with probability 5/6. There are $12 \times 2 = 24$ cubes with two painted faces and these show one painted face with probability 1/3. The other 16 cubes show one painted face with probability 0. So the probability that one painted face shows is
$P = (24/64) \times (5/6) + (24/64) \times (1/3) = 7/16$.

19. E.

Spot can go anywhere in a 252° sector of radius two yards and can cover a 72° sector of radius one yard around each of the adjoining corners. The total area is

$$\pi(2)^2 \times \frac{252}{360} + 2\left(\pi(1^2) \times \frac{72}{360}\right) = \frac{16\pi}{5}$$

20. A.

Let x and y be the sides of the triangles on the sides of the rectangle of lengths 23 and 37. Because all sides of the octagon are equal

$$\sqrt{x^2 + y^2} = 23 - 2x \qquad\qquad (1)$$
$$23 - 2x = 37 - 2y \qquad\qquad (2)$$

The second equation yields $y - x = 7$

Plugging into the first equation and squaring yields:

$$x^2 + (x+7)^2 = (23 - 2x)^2 \Rightarrow$$
$$x^2 + x^2 + 14x + 49 = 529 + 4x^2 - 92x$$
$$\Rightarrow 2x^2 - 106x + 480 = 0 \Rightarrow x^2 - 53x + 240 = 0$$
$$\Rightarrow (x - 5)(x - 48) = 0.$$

$x = 5$ or $x = 48$ (ignored since it is larger than 23)
The answer is $23 - 2x = 23 - 10 = 13$.

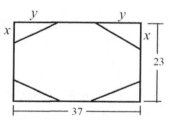

21. C.

Assume that Harry is in room # 5 and the seven girls are in rooms # 1 to # 4.
For girls, $7 = 2 + 2 + 2 + 1$
Number of girls that can be assigned to the rooms:

2   2   2   1

We have $\binom{7}{2} \times \binom{5}{2} \times \binom{3}{2} \times \binom{1}{1} \times \frac{4!}{3!} = 2520$ ways.

Since that Harry can be in room 5, 4, 3, 2, or 1, we have the final answer 2520×5 = 12600 ways.

22. D.

$2a^2 - 2ab + b^2 + 6a + 9 = 0 \quad \Rightarrow \quad (a^2 - 2ab + b^2) + (a^2 + 6a + 9) = 0 \quad \Rightarrow$

$(a-b)^2 + (a+3)^2 = 0.$

Since $(a-b)^2 \geq 0$ and $(a+3)^2 \geq 0$, $a-b=0$ and $a+3=0$.

We get $a = -3$ and $b = a = -3$.

$a^2 b + ab^2 = 2a^3 = 2(-3)^3 = -54$.

23. B.

Since $S_{\triangle BDE} = S_{\triangle DEC}$, $BD = DC$.

Since $S_{\triangle BCE} = 2S_{\triangle ACE}$, $BE = 2AE$.

So $\dfrac{S_{\triangle BCE}}{S_{\triangle ACE}} = \dfrac{BE}{AE} = 2$. Thus $S_{\triangle ADE} = \dfrac{1}{2} S_{\triangle BDE} = \dfrac{1}{2}(\dfrac{1}{3} S_{\triangle ABC}) = \dfrac{1}{2} \times \dfrac{1}{3} \times 36 = 6$.

24. A.

The sum of the two numbers chosen by Tina can be 3, 4, 5, 6, 7, 8, 9, 10, or 11.
Say that Tina picks up a number from the set {3, 4, 5, 6, 7, 8, 9, 10, 11} and
Sergio picks up a number from the set {1, 2, 3, 4, 5, 6, 7, 8, 9, 10, 11}.

Let B be the event that Sergio's number is smaller than Tina's number

A_1 be the event that Tina picks up the number 3

B_1 be the event that Sergio picks up a number that is smaller than Tina's number after A_1

A_2 be the event that Tina picks up the number 4

B_2 be the event that Sergio picks up a number that is smaller than Tina's number after A_2

A_3 be the event that Tina picks up the number 5

B_3 be the event that Sergio picks up a number that is smaller than Tina's number after A_3

A_4 be the event that Tina picks up the number 6

B_4 be the event that Sergio picks up a number that is smaller than Tina's number after A_4

A_5 be the event that Tina picks up the number 7

B_5 be the event that Sergio picks up a number that is smaller than Tina's number after A_4

A_6 be the event that Tina picks up the number 8

B_6 be the event that Sergio picks up a number that is smaller than Tina's number after A_5

A_7 be the event that Tina picks up the number 9

B_7 be the event that Sergio picks up a number that is smaller than Tina's number after A_6

A_8 be the event that Tina picks up the number 10

B_8 be the event that Sergio picks up a number that is smaller than Tina's number after A_6

A_9 be the event that Tina picks up the number 11

B_9 be the event that Sergio picks up a number that is smaller than Tina's number after A_6

Then $B = A_1B_1 + A_2B_2 + A_3B_3 + \ldots + A_9B_9$

$P(B) = P(A_1B_1) + P(A_2B_2) + P(A_3B_3) + \ldots + P(A_9B_9)$

$= P(A_1)P(B_1|A_1) + P(A_2)P(B_2|A_2) + P(A_3)P(B_3|A_3) + \ldots + P(B_9|A_9)$

We know that Tina has 1/9 of chance to pick up the number 3. So $P(A_1) = 1/9$. We know that when Tina picks up the number 3, Sergio can pick up the numbers 1 or 2 from the set $\{1, 2, 3, 4, 5, 6, 7, 8, 9, 10, 11\}$. So $P(B_1) = 2/11$.

Therefore $P(B) = \dfrac{1}{9} \times \dfrac{2}{11} + \dfrac{1}{9} \times \dfrac{3}{11} + \ldots + \dfrac{1}{9} \times \dfrac{10}{11} = \dfrac{1}{9} \times \dfrac{54}{11} = \dfrac{6}{11}$.

25. D.

We know that the areas of triangles ADO and BCO are the same.

So $S_{\triangle ADO} = S_{\triangle BCO} = \dfrac{40}{2} = 20$.

We also see that $\dfrac{S_{\triangle AOB}}{S_{\triangle BCO}} = \dfrac{AO}{OC} = \dfrac{S_{\triangle AOD}}{S_{\triangle DOC}}$ $\qquad \Rightarrow \qquad$ $\dfrac{5}{20} = \dfrac{20}{S_{\triangle DOC}}$ $\qquad \Rightarrow$

$$S_{\triangle DOC} = \dfrac{20 \times 20}{5} = 80.$$

The area of trapezoid $ABCD$ is $S_{\triangle AOB} + (S_{\triangle AOD} + S_{\triangle BOC}) + S_{\triangle DOC} = 5 + 40 + 80 = 125$.

American Mathematics Competitions

Practice 4
AMC 10

(American Mathematics Contest 10)

INSTRUCTIONS

1. This is a twenty-five question multiple choice test. Each question is followed by answers marked A, B, C, D and E. Only one of these is correct.

2. You will have 75 minutes to complete the test.

3. No aids are permitted other than scratch paper, graph paper, rulers, and erasers. No problems on the test will require the use of a calculator.

4. Figures are not necessarily drawn to scale.

5. SCORING: You will receive 6 points for each correct answer, 1.5 points for each problem left unanswered, and 0 points for each incorrect answer.

1. What is the difference between the sum of the first 2015 even counting numbers and the sum of the first 2015 odd counting numbers?

(A) 0   (B) 1   (C) 2   (D) 2015   (E) 4030

2. Members of the Little Soccer League buy socks and T–shirts. Socks cost $6 per pair and each T–shirt costs $6 more than a pair of socks. Each member needs one pair of socks and a shirt for home games and another pair of socks and a shirt for away games. If the total cost is $3312, how many members are in the League?

(A) 69   (B) 92   (C) 138   (D) 182   (E) 276

3. A solid box is 8 cm by 16 cm by 25 cm. A new solid is formed by removing a cube 4 cm on a side from each corner of this box. What percent of the original volume is removed?

(A) 5   (B) 9   (C) 12   (D) 16   (E) 20

4. It takes Betsy 40 minutes to walk uphill 2 km from her home to school, but it takes her only 20 minutes to walk from school to home along the same route. What is her average speed, in km/hr, for the round trip?

(A) 3   (B) 4   (C) 5   (D) 6   (E) 8

5. Let d and e denote the solutions of $2x^2 - 7x + 3 = 0$. What is the value of $(d + 1)(e + 1)$?

(A) 3   (B) 4   (C) 5   (D) 6   (E) 8

6. There are 20 posts on one side of a straight street. Alex walks with a constant speed from the first post to the last post. It takes him 6.6 seconds to walk from the first post to the 6th post. Find the time in seconds for him to reach the last post.

(A) 22   (B) 25.08   (C) 23.76   (D) 19.8   (E) 18.08

7. How many non-congruent triangles with perimeter 12 have integer side lengths?

(A) 1   (B) 2   (C) 3   (D) 4   (E) 5

8. What is the probability that a randomly selected positive factor of 100 is less than 21?

(A) 1/2   (B) 1/3   (C) 2/3   (D) 4/5   (E) 2/7

9. What is the greatest possible value of $a + b + c + d$ if the product $abcd$ is 6045? $a, b, c,$ and d are distinct positive integers.

(A) 52   (B) 76   (C) 112   (D) 172   (E) 412

10. In triangle ABC, $BC = 4$ cm, $AD = 3$ cm. The triangle ABC moves upward at the speed of 4 cm per seconds. What is the area swept by the triangle in 3 seconds?

(A) 36   (B) 54   (C) 108   (D) 112   (E) 114

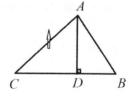

11. Find the value of n if $2^{90} + 2^{65} + 2^n$ is a square number.

(A) 22   (B) 34   (C) 38   (D) 40   (E) 90

12. A point (x, y) is randomly picked from inside the rectangle with vertices (0, 0), (8, 0), (8, 2), and (0, 2). What is the probability that $x > y$?

(A) 3/4   (B) 5/7   (C) 7/8   (D) 1/8   (E) 8/9

13. Find the sum of all possible values of a if both a and $\dfrac{39}{a^2 + a - 3}$ are positive integers.

(A) 14   (B) 12   (C) 8   (D) 7   (E) 6

14. Let m be the largest integer that is the product of exactly 3 distinct prime numbers, a, b and $20a + b$, where a and b are single digits. What is the sum of the digits of m?

(A) 13   (B) 16   (C) 18   (D) 19   (E) 21

15. A positive integer is randomly selected from all positive integers among 1 and 300 inclusive that are multiples of 3, 4, or 5. What is the probability that the positive integer selected is divisible by 5 only?

(A) 1/3   (B) 1/4   (C) 1/5   (D) 1/6   (E) 1/7

16. What is the units digit of 13^{2015}?

(A) 1   (B) 3   (C) 7   (D) 8   (E) 9

17. The number of inches in the perimeter of an equilateral triangle equals the number of square inches in the area of its inscribed circle. What is the radius, in inches, of the circle?

(A) $\dfrac{6\sqrt{2}}{\pi}$ (B) $\dfrac{6\sqrt{3}}{\pi}$ (C) $\dfrac{3\sqrt{3}}{\pi}$ (D) $\dfrac{6}{\pi}$ (E) 3π

18. What is the sum of the reciprocals of the roots of the equation $\dfrac{2015}{2016}x+1+\dfrac{1}{x}=0$?

(A) 1   (B) – 1   (C) $\dfrac{2016}{2015}$ (D) $-\dfrac{2016}{2015}$ (E) $-\dfrac{2015}{2016}$

19. A quarter circle of diameter 24 is shown. M is the center of a semicircle of diameter OB. $MP \parallel OA$ and meets the semicircle at N and the quarter circle at P. Determine S, the area of the shaded region.

(A) $9(\pi-\sqrt{3})$ (B) $12(\pi-\sqrt{3})$ (C) $15\pi-18\sqrt{3}$

(D) $18(\pi-\sqrt{3})$ (E) $9\sqrt{3}$.

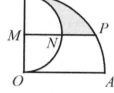

20. There are 52 students in a class. 30 of them can swim. 35 can ride bicycle. 42 can play table tennis. At least how many students can do all three sports?

(A) 2   (B) 3   (C) 6   (D) 10   (E) 17

21. The measure of each interior angle of a quadrilateral is a multiple of 24°. How many possible quadrilaterals are there that four angles are all distinct?

(A) 2   (B) 5   (C) 6   (D) 8   (E) 12

22. As shown in the figure, CD is the altitude on the side AB of right $\triangle ABC$. Find the value of $AC : BC$ if $AD : BD = \sqrt{3} : 1$.

(A) $\sqrt{3}$ (B) $\sqrt[3]{3}$ (C) $\sqrt[4]{3}$ (D) $\sqrt[4]{2}$ (E) $\sqrt[4]{5}$

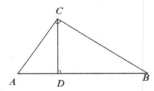

23. Figure 1 is a figure of a rectangle cutting into two triangles by its diagonal. There are 5 sides in Figure (1). Figure (2) has 16 sides, and Figure (3) has 33 sides. If the pattern continues, the number of sides in the 1001th figure is n. Find the sum of the digit of n.

(A) 8   (B) 16   (C) 24   (D) 32   (E) 40

(1)

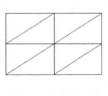

(2)

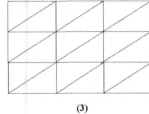

(3)

24. Mary has an infinite number of balls and empty boxes available to her. The empty boxes, each capable of holding three balls, are arranged in a row from right to left. At the first step, she places a ball in the first box of the row. At each subsequent step, she places a ball in the first box of the row that still has room for a ball and empties any previous boxes. How many balls in total are in the boxes as a result of Mary's 2016th step?

(A) 8   (B) 9   (C) 10   (D) 12   (E) 15

25. It is known that, for all positive integers k,
$$1^2 + 2^2 + 3^2 + \cdots + k^2 = \frac{k(k+1)(2k+1)}{6}.$$ Find the smallest positive integer k such that $1^2 + 2^2 + 3^2 + \cdots + k^2$ is a multiple of 100.

(A) 20   (B) 24   (C) 25   (D) 26   (E) none of the above

ANSWER KEYS

1. D.
2. B.
3. D.
4. B.
5. D.
6. B.
7. C.
8. C.
9. E.
10. B.
11. C.
12. C.
13. C.
14. D.
15. D.
16. C.
17. B.
18. B.
19. C.
20. B.
21. C.
22. C.
23. B.
24. B.
25. B.

SOLUTIONS:

1. D.
Each even counting number, beginning with 2, is one more than the pre ceding odd counting number. Therefore the difference is (1)(2015) = 2015.

2. B.
The cost for each member is the price of two pairs of socks, $12, and two shirts, $24, for a total of $36. So there are 3312/36 = 92 members.

3. D.
The total volume of the eight removed cubes is $8 \times 4^3 = 512$ cubic centimeters, and the volume of the original box is $8 \times 16 \times 25 = 3200$ cubic centimeters. Therefore the volume has been reduced by 512/3200 = 0.16 = 16%.

4. B.
Betsy walks a total of 4 km in 60 minutes or 1 hour. So her average speed, in km/hr, is 4/1 = 4.

5. D.
By Vieta's Theorem, $d + e = \dfrac{7}{2}$ and $d \times e = \dfrac{3}{2}$.

$(d + 1)(e + 1) = de + (d + e) + 1 = \dfrac{3}{2} + \dfrac{7}{2} + 1 = 6$.

6. B.
There are 5 intervals from the first post to the 6th post. Each interval takes 6.6/5 = 1.32 seconds. There are 19 intervals from the first post to the last post. 1.32 × 19 = 25.08 seconds.

7. C.
Let x denote the longest side. Then $x < \dfrac{1}{2} \times P = \dfrac{1}{2} \times 12 = 6$.

If $x = 5$, the other two sides have the length with the sum of 7. Possible combinations are: 5, 5, 2 and 5, 4, 3.

If $x = 4$, the other two sides have the sum of 8. The only possible way is 4, 4, 4 (since x is the longest side).

So in total there will be three such triangles.

8. C.

The factors of 100 are 1, 2, 4, 5, 10, 20, 25, 50, and 100. Six of the nine factors are less than 21, so the probability is 6/9 = 1/3.

9. E.

$abcd = 6045 = 3 \times 5 \times 13 \times 31 = 1 \times 3 \times 5 \times (13 \times 31)$.

The greatest sum will be $1 + 3 + 5 + 13 \times 31 = 412$.

10. B.

In 4 seconds, the side BC will move to the position of B_1C_1. The area of rectangle BCB_1C_1 is $4 \times 12 = 48$.

The area of triangle $A_1B_1C_1$ is $\dfrac{4 \times 3}{2} = 6$.

The answer is $48 + 6 = 54 \ cm^2$.

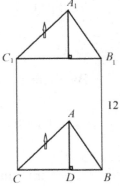

11. C.

$2^{90} + 2^{65} + 2^n = (2^{45})^2 + 2 \times 2^{45} \times 2^{19} + (2^{19})^2 - (2^{19})^2 + 2^n = (2^{45} + 2^{19})^2 - 2^{38} + 2^n$.

When n = 38, we see that $2^{90} + 2^{65} + 2^n = (2^{45} + 2^{19})^2 - 2^{38} + 2^{38} = (2^{45} + 2^{19})^2$ is a square number.

12. C.

The point (x, y) satisfies $x > y$ if and only if it belongs to the shaded triangle bounded by the lines $x = y$, $y = 2$, and $x = 8$, the area of which is $8 \times 2 - \dfrac{2 \times 2}{2} = 14$. The ratio of the area of the triangle to the area of the rectangle is $\dfrac{14}{16} = \dfrac{7}{8}$

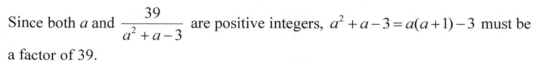

13. C.

Since both a and $\dfrac{39}{a^2 + a - 3}$ are positive integers, $a^2 + a - 3 = a(a+1) - 3$ must be a factor of 39.

Case 1: $a(a+1) = 39 + 3 = 42$

We know that $42 = 1 \times 42 = 2 \times 21 = 3 \times 14 = 6 \times 7$.

So $a = 6$.

Case 2: $a(a+1) = 13 + 3 = 16$.

16 cannot be written as the product of two consecutive integers.

Case 3: $a(a+1) = 3 + 3 = 6$

We know that $6 = 1 \times 6 = 2 \times 3$.

So $a = 2$.

Case 4: $a(a+1) = 1 + 3 = 4$.

4 cannot be written as the product of two consecutive integers.

So the answer is $6 + 2 = 8$.

14. (D).

The largest single-digit primes are 5 and 7. $20 \times 7 + 5 = 145$ is not a prime. $20 \times 5 + 7 = 107$ is a prime.

Using 5, 7, and 107 gives 3745, whose digits have a sum of 19.

15. D.

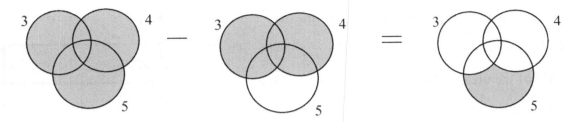

$$\left\lfloor \frac{300}{3} \right\rfloor + \left\lfloor \frac{300}{4} \right\rfloor + \left\lfloor \frac{300}{5} \right\rfloor - \left\lfloor \frac{300}{3\times 4} \right\rfloor - \left\lfloor \frac{300}{3\times 5} \right\rfloor - \left\lfloor \frac{300}{4\times 5} \right\rfloor + \left\lfloor \frac{300}{3\times 4\times 5} \right\rfloor$$

$$=100+75+60-25-20-15+5=180$$

$$\left\lfloor \frac{300}{3} \right\rfloor + \left\lfloor \frac{300}{4} \right\rfloor - \left\lfloor \frac{300}{3\times 4} \right\rfloor = 100+75-25=150$$

$$180 - 150 = 30.$$

The probability is $P = \dfrac{30}{180} = \dfrac{1}{6}$.

16. C.

The units digit of 13^{2015} is the same as the units digit of 3^{2015}.

Since the units digit of a^n repeats every fourth power, and $2015 = 503 \times 4 + 3$, the units digit of 3^{2015} is the same as the units digit of $3^3 = 27$, which is 7.

17. B.

We know that $S_\Delta = s \cdot r$, where $s = \dfrac{1}{2}(a+b+c)$, S_Δ is the area

of triangle ABC and r is the radius of its inscribed circle O.

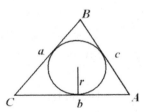

For an equilateral triangle, $a = b = c$ and $S_\Delta = \dfrac{\sqrt{3}}{4} a^2$.

So we have $\dfrac{\sqrt{3}}{4} a^2 = \dfrac{3a}{2} \times r \quad \Rightarrow \quad \dfrac{\sqrt{3}}{2} a = 3r$ (1)

We are given that $3a = \pi \times r^2$ (2)

(2) ÷ (1): $\dfrac{3a}{\dfrac{\sqrt{3}}{2}a} = \dfrac{\pi \times r^2}{3r}$ $\Rightarrow$ $\dfrac{6}{\sqrt{3}} = \dfrac{\pi \times r}{3}$ $\Rightarrow$ $r = \dfrac{18}{\pi\sqrt{3}} = \dfrac{6\sqrt{3}}{\pi}$.

18. B.

Multiplying both sides of the given equation by x: $\dfrac{2015}{2016}x^2 + x + 1 = 0$.

If the roots of this equation are denoted r and s, then by Vieta's Theorem,

$$r + s = -\dfrac{1}{\dfrac{2015}{2016}} = -\dfrac{2016}{2015} \qquad\qquad (1)$$

$$rs = \dfrac{1}{\dfrac{2015}{2016}} = \dfrac{2016}{2015} \qquad\qquad (2)$$

The sum of the reciprocals of the roots of the equation is

$$\dfrac{1}{r} + \dfrac{1}{s} = \dfrac{r + s}{rs} = \dfrac{-\dfrac{2016}{2015}}{\dfrac{2016}{2015}} = -1.$$

19. C.

Connect OP. In right triangle OMP, $OM = \dfrac{1}{2}OB = \dfrac{1}{2}OP$.

So $\angle OPM = 30°$ and $\angle POB = 60°$.

The area of the shaded region = the area of the sector S_{POB} – the

area of the sector S_{NMB} – the area of the right triangle POM $S_{\triangle POM}$

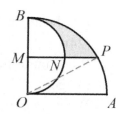

$= \dfrac{60°}{360°} \times \pi \times 12^2 - \dfrac{90°}{360°} \times \pi \times 6^2 - \dfrac{6 \times 6\sqrt{3}}{2} = 24\pi - 9\pi - 18\sqrt{3} = 15\pi - 18\sqrt{3}$.

20. B.
Method 1: Number of students who cannot swim: $52 - 30 = 22$.
Number of students who cannot ride bicycle: $52 - 35 = 17$.
Number of students who cannot play tennis: $52 - 42 = 10$.
At most $22 + 17 + 10 = 49$ students cannot play at least one of the three activities.
At least $52 - 49 = 3$ students can do all three sports.

Method 2: **The tickets method**
Step 1: Give each student a ticket for each activity he or she likes. $30 + 35 + 42 = 107$ tickets are given out.

Step 2: Take away the tickets from them. Students who have 2 or more tickets will give back 2 tickets. Students who have less than 2 tickets will give back all the tickets.

Step 3: Calculate the number of tickets taken back: at most $2 \times 52 = 104$ tickets were taken back.
Step 4: Calculate the number of tickets that are still in the students hands. $107 - 104 = 3$.
At this moment, any student who has the ticket will have only one ticket. These students are the ones who like 3 activities. The answer is 3

21. C.
Let the angles be $24w$, $24x$, $24y$, $24z$. x, y, and z are all distinct positive integers.
$(24w + 24x + 24y + 24z) = 360° \qquad \Rightarrow \qquad w + x + y + z = 15$.
We want to find the number of ways to write 15 as the sum of 4 distinct positive integers.
We have two methods:
Method 1:
Find $Q(15,4)$.

W know that $Q(n,k) = P\left(n - \binom{k}{2}, k\right) \Rightarrow \quad Q(15,4) = P\left(15 - \binom{4}{2}, 4\right) = P(9,4)$

$P(n+k,k) = P(n,1) + P(n,2) + \ldots + P(n,k)$

$P(5+4,4) = P(5,1) + P(5,2) + P(5,3) + P(5,4) = 1 + \left\lfloor \frac{5}{2} \right\rfloor + \left\lfloor \frac{5^2}{12} \right\rfloor + 1 = 1 + 2 + 2$

$+ 1 = 6.$

Method 2: By listing.

(1, 2, 3, 9), (1, 2, 4, 8), (1, 2, 5, 7), (1, 3, 4, 7), (1, 3, 5, 6), and (2, 3, 4, 6).

The answer is 6.

22. C.

Since all the triangles are similar, we have

$AC^2 = AB \times AD$ $\qquad\qquad$ (1)

$BC^2 = AB \times BD$ $\qquad\qquad$ (2)

(1) ÷ (2): $\dfrac{AC^2}{BC^2} = \dfrac{AB \times AD}{AB \times BD} = \dfrac{AD}{BD} = \sqrt{3} \qquad \Rightarrow \dfrac{AC}{BC} = \sqrt[4]{3}.$

23. B.

$a_{100} = 5\binom{1001-1}{0} + 11\binom{1001-1}{1} + 6\binom{1001-1}{2} = 5 + 11 \times 1000 + 6 \times 500 \times 999$

$= 3008005.$

The sum of the digits is $3 + 8 + 5 = 16.$

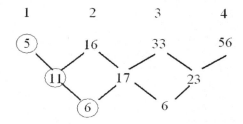

24. B.

After trying the first few steps, we notice that the boxes resemble the set of positive integers in base 4.

Step 1 | 1
2 | 2
3 | 3
4 | 1 | 0

Step 5 | 1 | 1
6 | 1 | 2
7 | 1 | 3
8 | 2 | 0

Step 9 | 2 | 1
10 | 2 | 2
11 | 2 | 3
12 | 3 | 0

Step 13 | 3 | 1
14 | 3 | 2
15 | 3 | 3
16 | 1 | 0 | 0

Since $2016_{10} = 133200_4$, we know that we have $1 + 3 + 3 + 2 + 0 + 0 = 9$ balls.

25. B.

The sum is a multiple of 100 if and only if $k(k + 1)(2k + 1) = 6 \times 100N = 2^3 \times 3 \times 5N$ for some positive integer N. Because $2k + 1$ is odd and k and $k + 1$ cannot both be even, it follows that either k or $k + 1$ is a multiple of 8 (we have taken care of 2^3 in the factors $2^3 \times 3 \times 5N$) . Furthermore, the product is divisible by 6 then divisible by 3 for all integer values of k (we have taken care of 3 in the factors $2^3 \times 3 \times 5N$). $k = 8, 9, 16, 17, 24, 25, \ldots$ We see that when $k = 24$, $k(k + 1)(2k + 1)$ is divisible by 25 (we have taken care of 5^2 in the factors $2^3 \times 3 \times 5N$). So 24 is the smallest positive integer for which $k(k + 1)(2k + 1)$ is a multiple of 100.

American Mathematics Competitions

Practice 5
AMC 10

(American Mathematics Contest 10)

INSTRUCTIONS

1. This is a twenty-five question multiple choice test. Each question is followed by answers marked A, B, C, D and E. Only one of these is correct.

2. You will have 75 minutes to complete the test.

3. No aids are permitted other than scratch paper, graph paper, rulers, and erasers. No problems on the test will require the use of a calculator.

4. Figures are not necessarily drawn to scale.

5. SCORING: You will receive 6 points for each correct answer, 1.5 points for each problem left unanswered, and 0 points for each incorrect answer.

1. You and six friends need to raise $1400 in donations for a charity, dividing the fundraising equally. How many dollars will each of you need to raise?

(A) 200   (B) 300   (C) 400   (D) 700   (E) 1400

2. How many two-digit positive integers have at least one 5 as a digit?

(A) 90   (B) 18   (C) 19   (D) 20   (E) 72

3. A standard six-sided die is rolled. P is the product and S is the sum of the five numbers that are visible, respectively. What is the largest possible ratio of P/S?

(A) 48   (B) 20   (C) 36   (D) 10   (E) 8

4. What is the value of x if $|x - 2| = |x - 5|$?

(A) 3/2   (B) 5/2   (C) 7/2   (D) 2   (E) 3

5. A set of four points is chosen randomly from the grid shown. Each four-point set has the same probability of being chosen. What is the probability that the points lie on the same straight line?

(A) 2/455   (B) 1/182   (C) 1/455   (D) 1/91   (E) 1/2

6. A frog is going to hop up the stairs from the first floor to the second floor. Hopping up the stairs one step at a time will require a total of ten hops. If the frog

can hop two, three, or four steps at a time, how many different sequences of hops are possible for the frog to reach the second floor with each hop being upward?

(A) 5   (B) 7   (C) 12   (D) 17   (E) 26

7. A grocer stacks oranges in a pyramid-like stack with a rectangular base. Each orange above the bottom level rests in a pocket formed by four oranges in the level below. The stack is completed by a single row of m oranges on the top layer, $2(m + 1)$ oranges on the second layer, $3(m + 2)$ on the third layer, $4(m + 3)$ on the fourth layer,…. How many oranges are in the stack if the total number of layers is 11 with $m = 2$?

(A) 440   (B) 572   (C) 612   (D) 717   (E) 726

8. A Fibonacci sequence is defined by $F_n = F_{n-1} + F_{n-2}$ for $n > 1$ with $F_0 = 1$ and $F_1 = 1$.
The first several Fibonacci numbers are 1, 1, 2, 3, 5, 8, 13, 21, 34, 55, 89, 144, ….
Find the remainder when the 2015th term in the sequence is divided by 5.

(A) 0   (B) 1   (C) 2   (D) 3   (E) 4

9. In square $ABCD$, $AB = 4$. Sectors ABD and DAC are quarter circles. Two shaded areas are the same. Find the positive difference of the two unshaded areas.

(A) $8\pi - 16$.   (B) $16\pi - 8$.   (C) $4\pi + 16$.
(D) $8\pi + 8$.   (E) $4\pi + 8$.

10. Alex flipped a coin three times and Bob then flipped the same coin three times. What is the probability that the number of heads obtained by Alex is more than that the number of heads obtained by Bob?

(A) 5/16   (B) 25/64   (C) 11/32   (D) 23/64   (E) 1/2

11. A square pyramid has a base edge of 64 inches and an altitude of 1 foot. A square pyramid whose altitude is one-fourth of the original altitude is cut away at the vertex. The volume of the remaining frustum is what fractional part of the volume of the original pyramid?

A. $\dfrac{63}{64}$.   B. $\dfrac{31}{32}$.   C. $\dfrac{15}{16}$.   D. $\dfrac{3}{4}$.   E. $\dfrac{1}{64}$.

12. In how many ways can three people divide among themselves eight identical apples, three identical oranges, two identical plums, and one tangerine (without cutting any fruit)?

(A) 2400   (B) 2700   (C) 7680   (D) 8100   (E) 48

13. At a party, each man danced with exactly four women and each woman danced with exactly three men. Fifteen men attended the party. How many women attended the party?

(A) 27   (B) 24   (C) 22   (D) 20   (E) 15

14. The average value of all the pennies, nickels, dimes, and quarters in Paul's wallet is 21 cents. If he had five more quarters, the average value would be 23 cents. How many pennies does he have in his wallet?

(A) 0   (B) 1   (C) 2   (D) 3   (E) 4

15. Given that $1/3 \leq x \leq 4$, find the greatest possible value of $y = \dfrac{\sqrt{13x - 4}}{x}$.

A. $\dfrac{169}{16}$.   B. $\dfrac{13}{4}$.   C. 3.   D. $\dfrac{225}{16}$.   E. $\dfrac{\sqrt{13}}{2}$.

16. The 4×6 rectangular grid of squares shown below contains a shaded square. What is the probability that a randomly selected rectangular sub-region contains the shaded area?

(A) 2/7   (B) 5/6   (C) 1/3   (D) 3/7   (E) 3/8

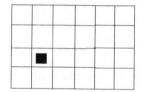

17. As shown in the figure, AB is the diameter of the circular path. Alex starts to run at point A, Bob starts to run at point B, at the same time but opposite direction. They first meet at point C. The length of the path from C to A is 100 meters. They next meet at point D. The length of the path from D to B is 80 meters. Find the circumference of the circle.

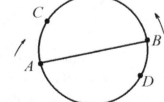

(A) 250   (B) 300   (C) 350   (D) 440   (E) 500

18. If the number 783 is divisible by 257 in base b, find the value of b.

(A) 2   (B) 3   (C) 6   (D) 9   (E) 11

19. A white cylindrical silo has a diameter of 20 feet and a height of 60 feet. A red stripe with a horizontal width of 3 feet is painted on the silo, as shown, making two complete revolutions around it. What is the area of the stripe in square feet?

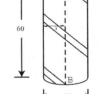

(A) 360   (B) 180   (C) 240   (D) 260   (E) 380

20. *ABCD* is a rectangle. *E* is a point on *BC* and *F* is a point on *CD*. The areas of the triangles *ABE, ECF,* and *FDA* are 4, 3, and 5, respectively. What is the area of the triangle *AEF*?

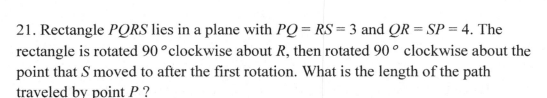

(A) 4   (B) 6   (C) 7   (D) 8   (E) 10

21. Rectangle *PQRS* lies in a plane with $PQ = RS = 3$ and $QR = SP = 4$. The rectangle is rotated $90°$ clockwise about *R*, then rotated $90°$ clockwise about the point that *S* moved to after the first rotation. What is the length of the path traveled by point *P* ?

(A) $(\sqrt{2}+\sqrt{5})\pi$ (B) 6π (C) $\dfrac{9}{2}\pi$ (D) $(\sqrt{3}+2)\pi$ (E) $2\sqrt{10}\pi$

22. Square *ABCD* has side length 4. A semicircle with diameter *AB* is constructed inside the square, and the tangent to the semicircle from *C* intersects side *AD* at *E*. What is the length of *AE*?

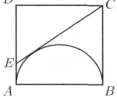

(A) 1/2   (B) 1   (C) 3/20   (D) 2   (E) 3

23. A pentagon is made up of an equilateral triangle ABC of side length 2 on top of a square $BCDE$. Circumscribe a circle through points A, D and E. Find the radius of the circle.

(A) 3   (B) 1   (C) 2   (D) 6   (E) 40

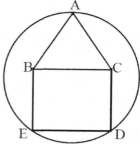

24. Alex wants to select two different numbers from $\{2, 3, 4, 5, 6, 7, 8, 9\}$. How many ways are there to do so such that these two numbers are not consecutive?

(A) 36   (B) 21   (C) 24   (D) 26   (E) 38

25. K is the set of natural numbers with the property that every element in K is not divisible by 3 and is not divisible by 4. But if a number is divisible by 3 or 4 and is also divisible by 5, the number is in K (like 15, 20, 60,…).. Find the 79th smallest member of K.

(A) 260   (B) 180   (C) 140   (D) 160   (E) 133

ANSWER KEYS

1. A.
2. B.
3. C.
4. C.
5. B.
6. D.
7. B.
8. A.
9. A.
10. C.
11. A.
12. D.
13. D.
14. A.
15. B.
16. A.
17. D.
18. D.
19. B.
20. D.
21. C.
22. B.
23. C.
24. B.
25. E.

When $m = 2$ and $n = 11$, we get $\frac{1}{6}n(n+1)(2n+3m-2) =$

$\frac{1}{6} \times 11(11+1)(2 \times 11 + 3 \times 2 - 2) = 572.$

Method 2:

Number of layers: 1   2   3   4

Number of oranges: 2   6   12   20

                         4   6   8

                            2   2

By Newton's Little Formula, the Sum of the n terms

$$S_n = 0 \times \binom{n}{0} + A \times \binom{n}{1} + B \times \binom{n}{2} + C \times \binom{n}{3} + \ldots + K \times \binom{n}{m+1}$$

$$= 0 \times \binom{11}{0} + 2\binom{11}{1} + 4\binom{11}{2} + 2\binom{11}{3} = 0 + 2 \times 11 + 4 \times 11 \times 5 + 2 \times 11 \times 5 \times 3 = 572.$$

8. A.

$F_n = F_{n-1} + F_{n-2} = F_{n-1} + 2F_{n-3} + F_{n-4} = F_{n-3} + F_{n-4} + 2F_{n-4} + 2F_{n-5} + F_{n-4}$

$= 5F_{n-4} + 3F_{n-5}.$

We know that $F_5 = 5$. Thus every fifth term is divisible by 5.

$2015 = 5 \times 403$. So the remainder is 0 when the 2015th term in the sequence is divided by 5.

9. A.

The areas of S_1 and S form the quarter circle:

$S_1 + S = \frac{\pi \times 4^2}{4} = 4\pi \implies S_1 = 4\pi - S$ (1)

The areas of S_2 and S is obtained by subtracting the quarter circle from the square:

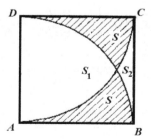

$S_2 + S = 16 - 4\pi \quad \Rightarrow \quad S_2 = 16 - S - 4\pi$ \hfill (2)

Therefore, the difference of the unshaded areas is (1) – (2):

$S_1 - S_2 = (4\pi - S) - (16 - S - 4\pi) = 8\pi - 16.$

10. C.

We have the following cases:

Alex	HTT	HHT	HHH
Bob	TTT	TTT, TTH	TTT, TTH, THH

The probability is

$P = (\dfrac{1}{2^3} \times \dfrac{3!}{2!}) \times (\dfrac{1}{2^3})$

$+ (\dfrac{1}{2^3} \times \dfrac{3!}{2!}) \times (\dfrac{1}{2^3} + \dfrac{1}{2^3} \times \dfrac{3!}{2!})$

$+ (\dfrac{1}{2^3}) \times (\dfrac{1}{2^3} + \dfrac{1}{2^3} \times \dfrac{3!}{2!} + \dfrac{1}{2^3} \times \dfrac{3!}{2!})$

$= \dfrac{3}{2^6} + \dfrac{12}{2^6} + \dfrac{7}{2^6} = \dfrac{22}{2^6} = \dfrac{11}{32}.$

11. A.

Let V_1 be the volume of the original pyramid and V_2 be the volume of the smaller pyramid that was sliced off.

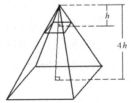

Since the original pyramid is similar to the smaller pyramid that was sliced off, the ratio of their volumes is equal to the cube of the ratio of their heights.

We have $\dfrac{V_2}{V_1} = \left(\dfrac{h}{4h} \right)^3 = \dfrac{1}{64}.$

The answer will be: $\dfrac{V_1 - V_2}{V_1} = 1 - \dfrac{V_2}{V_1} = 1 - \dfrac{1}{64} = \dfrac{63}{64}.$

12. D.

We divide the process of the distribution of the fruit into to four steps: apples, oranges, plums, and tangerine:

$$x + y + z = 8 \quad \Rightarrow \quad \binom{8+3-1}{3-1} = \binom{10}{2} = 5 \times 9 = 45$$

$$x + y + z = 3 \quad \Rightarrow \quad \binom{3+3-1}{3-1} = \binom{5}{2} = 10$$

$$x + y + z = 2 \quad \Rightarrow \quad \binom{2+3-1}{3-1} = \binom{4}{2} = 6$$

$$x + y + z = 1 \quad \Rightarrow \quad \binom{1+3-1}{3-1} = \binom{3}{2} = 3.$$

The answer is $45 \times 10 \times 6 \times 3 = 8100$.

13. D.

Because each man danced with exactly three women, there were $(15)(4) = 60$ pairs of men and women who danced together. Each woman had three partners, so the number of women who attended is $60/3 = 20$.

14. A.

If m is the number of coins in Paul's wallet, then their total value is $21m$ cents. If he had five more quarters, he would have $m + 5$ coins whose total value in cents could be expressed both as $21m + 25 \times 5$ and as $23(m + 5)$. Therefore

$21m + 25 \times 5 = 23(m + 5)$. So $m = 5$.

Since Paul has five coins with a total value of $21 \times 5 = 105$ cents, he must have four quarters and one nickel, so the number of dimes is 0.

15. B.

We know that $x > 0$. So $y = \dfrac{\sqrt{13x - 4}}{x} = \sqrt{\dfrac{13x - 4}{x^2}} = \sqrt{-4(\dfrac{1}{x^2}) + 13(\dfrac{1}{x})}$

$$= \sqrt{-4(\frac{1}{x} - \frac{13}{8})^2 + \frac{169}{16}} \, .$$

Since $(\frac{1}{x} - \frac{13}{8})^2 \geq 0$, the greatest possible value of y is $\sqrt{\frac{169}{16}} = \frac{13}{4}$ when $x = \frac{8}{13}$.

16. A.

The total number of rectangles equals $\binom{7}{2} \times \binom{5}{2} = 210$.

The number of rectangular sub-regions that contain the shaded area is $\binom{2}{1} \times \binom{5}{1} \times \binom{3}{1} \times \binom{2}{1} = 60$

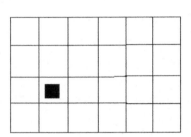

The probability equals 60/210= 2/7.

17. D.
When they first meet, they have run a distance of half the length of the circle. When they next meet, they have run a distance of whole circle. Therefore, the distance of $A - C - B - D$ is three times the distance of the path of $A - C$, or $100 \times 3 = 300$ meters, so the half circle has the length of $300 - 80 = 220$ meters. The circumference of the circle is then 2 $\times 220 = 440$ meters.

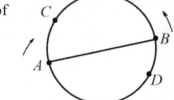

18. D.
We know that $b \geq 9$.
In any base $b \geq 9$, we have
$2 \times 257 < 2 \times 300 = 600 < 783 < 800 < 4 \times 200 < 4 \times 257$.
Therefore $783 = 3 \times 257$.
$7b^2 + 8b + 3 = 3(2b^2 + 5b + 7) \Rightarrow \qquad b^2 - 7b - 18 = 0 \qquad \Rightarrow$
$\qquad (b-9)(b+2) = 0$.
Solving for b: $b = 9$

19. B.

If the stripe were cut from the silo and spread flat, it would form a parallelogram 3 feet wide and 60 feet high. So the area of the stripe is 3(60) = 180 square feet.

 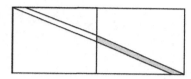

20. D.

Method 1: $S_{\triangle FDA} = 5$, so $AD = x$, $DF = 10/x$.

$S_{\triangle ADE} = 4$, so $AB = y$, $BE = 8/y$

Thus $CE = x - 8/y$ and $CF = y - 10/x$.

Using $CE \times CF = 6$, we have $xy + 80/(xy) = 24$.

It follows that $xy = 20$ or 4, but 4 is clearly not feasible in this problem.

Method 2:

Connect AC. Let $S_{\triangle AEC} = x$ and $S_{\triangle CAF} = y$.

We have $x + 4 = y + 5$ or

$x = y + 1$ (1)

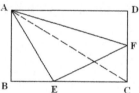

The ratio of the areas of 2 triangles with the same height is equal to the ratio of the bases.

In $\triangle ABC$ and $\triangle AEC$, $\dfrac{x+4}{x} = \dfrac{BC}{EC}$

In $\triangle ACF$ and $\triangle ECF$, $\dfrac{y}{3} = \dfrac{AD}{EC}$

Since $AD = BC$, $\dfrac{x+4}{x} = \dfrac{y}{3}$ (2)

Solve x and y in (1) and (2): $x = 6$ and $y = 5$.

$S_{\triangle AEF} = x + y - 3 = 8$

Method 3:

In rectangle $ABCD$, we have: $S_{ABCD} = 2S_{\triangle AEF} + BE \times DF$.

Then: $3 + 4 + 5 + S = 2S + BE \times DF \quad \Rightarrow \quad 12 = S + \dfrac{BE \times AB}{AB} \times \dfrac{DF \times AD}{AD}$

$\Rightarrow \quad 12 = S + \dfrac{2S_{\triangle ABE} \times 2S_{\triangle FDA}}{S_{ABCD}} \Rightarrow 12 = S + \dfrac{8 \times 10}{12 + S} \qquad \Rightarrow \qquad S = 8$.

21. C.

Let P' and S' denote the positions of P and S, respectively, after the rotation about R, and let P'' denote the final position of P. In the rotation that moves P to position P', the point P rotates 90° on a circle with center R and radius $PR = \sqrt{3^2 + 4^2} = 5$. The length of the arc traced by P is $\dfrac{1}{4}(2\pi \times 5) = \dfrac{5\pi}{2}$. Next, P' rotates to P' through a 90° arc on a circle with center S' and radius $S'P' = 4$. The length of this arc is $\dfrac{1}{4}(2\pi \times 4) = 2\pi$.

The total distance traveled by P is $\dfrac{5\pi}{2} + 2\pi = \dfrac{9}{2}\pi$.

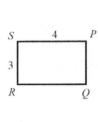 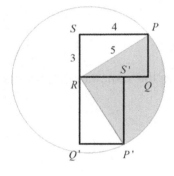 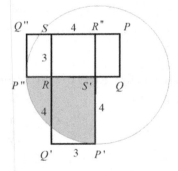

22. B.
Method 1:
 Let F be the point at which CE is tangent to the semicircle and let $AE = x$. Because CF and CB are both tangents to the semicircle, $CF = CB = 2$.

Similarly, $EA = EF = x$.
The Pythagorean Theorem applied to $\triangle CDE$ gives

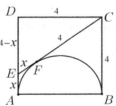

$(4-x)^2 + 4^2 = (4+x)^2$.
It follows that $x = 1$.

Method 2:

Connect GF. G is the center of the circle.
Quadrilaterals $BCFG$ and $FGAE$ are similar.

So we have $\dfrac{BC}{FG} = \dfrac{BG}{EF} \Rightarrow \dfrac{4}{2} = \dfrac{2}{x} \Rightarrow x = 1$.

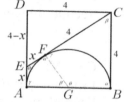

23. C.

Draw $AG \perp ED$. AG is the diameter.

Triangle ABE is a 30°-60°-90° triangle and $AE = \sqrt{3}$.

By the power of point theorem, $AF \times FG = EF \times FD$

$\Rightarrow \qquad (\sqrt{3} + 2) \times FG = 1 \times 1$

$FG = \dfrac{1}{(\sqrt{3}+2)} = \dfrac{(2-\sqrt{3})}{(2+\sqrt{3})(2-\sqrt{3})} = 2 - \sqrt{3}$.

So the diameter is $(\sqrt{3}+2) + 2 - \sqrt{3} = 4$.

The radius of the circle is 2.

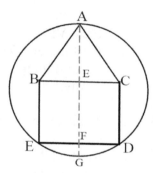

24. B.
Method 1 (Listing):

Case I:
First integer: 2
Second integer: 4, 5, 6, 7, 8, or 9
6 ways.

Case II:
First integer: 3
Second integer: 5, 6, 7, 8, or 9
5 ways.

Case III:
First integer: 4

Second integer: 6, 7, 8, or 9
4 ways.

Case IV:
First integer: 5
Second integer: 7, 8, or 9
3 ways.

Case V:
First integer: 6
Second integer: 8 or 9
2 ways.

Case VI:
First integer: 7
Second integer: 9
1 way.

Total $6 + 5 + 4 + 3 + 2 + 1 = 21$ ways.

Method 2:
The number of ways to select k non-consecutive elements from n consecutive
terms is $N = \dbinom{n - (k-1)}{k}$.

n is the total number of terms.
k is the number of elements selected.

$n = 9 - 2 + 1 = 8$. $k = 2$.

$$N = \binom{n - (k-1)}{k} = \binom{8 - (2-1)}{k} = \binom{7}{2} = 21.$$

25. E.
Method 1:
Let $a_{79} = n$.

$$79 = n - n(A \cup B) + n(A \cap C) + n(B \cap C) - n(A \cap B \cap C)$$

$$= n - \left\lfloor \frac{n}{3} \right\rfloor - \left\lfloor \frac{n}{4} \right\rfloor + \left\lfloor \frac{n}{3 \times 4} \right\rfloor + \left\lfloor \frac{n}{3 \times 5} \right\rfloor + \left\lfloor \frac{n}{4 \times 5} \right\rfloor - \left\lfloor \frac{n}{3 \times 4 \times 5} \right\rfloor \qquad (1)$$

We know that $x - 1 < \lfloor x \rfloor \le x$.

So $79 < n - (\frac{n}{3} - 1) - (\frac{n}{4} - 1) + \frac{n}{3 \times 4} + \frac{n}{3 \times 5} + \frac{n}{4 \times 5} - (\frac{n}{3 \times 4 \times 5} - 1) = \frac{3}{5}n + 3 \qquad (2)$

and $79 > n - \frac{n}{3} - \frac{n}{4} + (\frac{n}{3 \times 4} - 1) + (\frac{n}{3 \times 5} - 1) + (\frac{n}{4 \times 5} - 1) - \frac{n}{3 \times 4 \times 5} = \frac{3}{5}n - 3 \qquad (3)$

From (2) and (3) we get $126\frac{2}{3} < n < 136\frac{2}{3}$ or $127 \le n \le 136$.

We know that n is neither a multiple of 3 nor 4 (except a multiple of 5), so n must be one of 127, 130, 131, 133, 134, 135.

Substituting these possible values into (1), we see that the only solution is $n = 133$.

Method 2:

The least common multiple of 3, 4, and 5 is 60.

$$60 - \left\lfloor \frac{60}{3} \right\rfloor - \left\lfloor \frac{60}{4} \right\rfloor + \left\lfloor \frac{60}{3 \times 4} \right\rfloor + \left\lfloor \frac{60}{3 \times 5} \right\rfloor + \left\lfloor \frac{60}{4 \times 5} \right\rfloor - \left\lfloor \frac{60}{3 \times 4 \times 5} \right\rfloor = 36.$$

There are 36 terms in a_n from 1 to 60.

$a_1 = 1$, $a_2 = 2$, $a_3 = 5$, $a_4 = 7$, $a_5 = 10$, $a_6 = 11$ $a_7 = 13$, ..., $a_{36} = 60$.

We know that $79 = 36 \times 2 + 7$. So $a_{79} = 60 \times 2 + a_7 = 120 + 13 = 133$.

American Mathematics Competitions

Practice 6
AMC 10

(American Mathematics Contest 10)

INSTRUCTIONS

1. This is a twenty-five question multiple choice test. Each question is followed by answers marked A, B, C, D and E. Only one of these is correct.

2. You will have 75 minutes to complete the test.

3. No aids are permitted other than scratch paper, graph paper, rulers, and erasers. No problems on the test will require the use of a calculator.

4. Figures are not necessarily drawn to scale.

5. SCORING: You will receive 6 points for each correct answer, 1.5 points for each problem left unanswered, and 0 points for each incorrect answer.

1. A scout troop buys 2015 candy bars at a price of sixty-five for \$31. They sell all the candy bars at a price of thirteen for \$10. What was their profit, in dollars?

(A) 180   (B) 290   (C) 370   (D) 498   (E) 589

2. A positive number x has the property that $x\%$ of x is 729. What is x?

(A) 230   (B) 270   (C) 310   (D) 420   (E) 440

3. A gallon of paint is used to paint a room. Two third of the paint is used on the first day. On the second day, two fifth of the remaining paint is used. What fraction of the original amount of paint is available to use on the third day?

(A) $\dfrac{1}{3}$ (B) $\dfrac{1}{4}$ (C) $\dfrac{1}{5}$ (D) $\dfrac{1}{6}$ (E) $\dfrac{1}{15}$

4. A rectangle with a diagonal of length x is three fourth as long as it is wide. What is the perimeter of the rectangle?

(A) $\dfrac{11}{5}x$ (B) $\dfrac{14}{5}x$ (C) $\dfrac{12}{5}x$ (D) $3x$

(E) $\dfrac{14}{15}$

5. Alex, Bob, Cathy are seating with their friends around a circular table. Counting clockwise from Alex, Bob's number is 13. Counting counterclockwise from Alex, Cathy's number is 15. Counting clockwise from Cathy, Bob's number is 7. How many people are seating around the table?

(A) 13   (B) 15   (C) 18   (D) 19   (E) 20

6. Find the sum of all the prime factors of 1000027.
(A) 113   (B) 154   (C) 176   (D) 202   (E) 234

7. One die has faces 1, 1, 2, 4, 5, 5 and another has faces 2, 3, 4, 5, 6, 6. The dice are rolled and the numbers on the top faces are added. What is the probability that the sum will be even?

(A) $\dfrac{1}{3}$ (B) $\dfrac{2}{9}$ (C) $\dfrac{4}{9}$ (D) $\dfrac{1}{6}$ (E) $\dfrac{1}{15}$

8. The two tangent circles with the radii 3 and 1, respectively, have an external common tangent as shown. Find the shaded area.

(A) $4\sqrt{3} - \dfrac{11}{6}\pi$ (B) $4\sqrt{3}$ (C) $\dfrac{11}{6}\pi$ (D) 2π

(E) $4\sqrt{3} - \dfrac{7}{6}\pi$

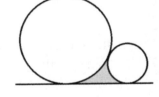

9. The first term of a sequence is 2017. Each succeeding term is the sum of the cubes of the digits of the previous term. What is the 2015th term of the sequence?

(A) 17   (B) 15   (C) 160   (D) 217   (E) 352

10. If a six-digit number $\overline{abcde\,8}$ is divided by 2, a new six-digit number is obtained as $\overline{2abcde}$. Find the sum of the digits of the original six-digit number $\overline{abcde\,8}$.

(A) 49   (B) 48   (C) 47   (D) 42   (E) 35

11. If ten coins are tossed, what is the probability that exactly five of them show heads and five of them show tails?

(A) $\dfrac{63}{256}$ (B) $\dfrac{6}{25}$ (C) $\dfrac{3}{16}$ (D) $\dfrac{1}{8}$ (E) $\dfrac{1}{4}$

12. Car A and car B travel toward each other at the same time. If car A started traveling x minutes earlier, the two cars would meet 30 minutes earlier than usual. Car A's speed is 60 km/h, Car B's speed is 40 km/h. What is x?

(A) 30   (B) 40   (C) 50   (D) 20   (E) 44

13. An envelope contains ten bills: 2 ones, 2 fives, 2 tens, 2 twenties and 2 thirties. Three bills are drawn at random without replacement. What is the probability that their sum is $50 or more?

(A) $\dfrac{39}{120}$ (B) $\dfrac{41}{120}\dfrac{1}{3}$ (C) $\dfrac{2}{9}$ (D) $\dfrac{1}{3}$ (E) $\dfrac{1}{15}$

14. How many positive integers n satisfy the following condition: $(8\sqrt{2}\,n)^{1000} > n^{1500} > 2^{3000}$?

(A) 1   (B) 8   (C) 32   (D) 64   (E) 123.

15. How many positive cubes divide $2^4 \times 3^6 \times 5^{10} \times 7^9$?

(A) 42   (B) 53   (C) 64   (D) 96   (E) 6

16. The sum of the digits of a three-digit number is subtracted from the number. The units digit of the result is 7. How many three-digit numbers less than 500 have this property?

(A) 35   (B) 37   (C) 40   (D) 50   (E) 60

17. For how many positive integers n less than or equal to 100 is $n!$ evenly divisible by $1 + 2 + \cdots + n$?

(A) 2   (B) 24   (C) 25   (D) 67   (E) 75

18. An arithmetic sequence with first term 1 has a common difference of 6. A second sequence begins with 4 and has a common difference of 7. In the range of 1 to 2015, find the number of terms common to both sequences.

(A) 35   (B) 37   (C) 48   (D) 50   (E) 60

19. A line parallel to the base of a triangle cuts the triangle into two regions of equal area. This line also cuts the altitude into two parts. Find

$$\frac{AG}{GD}.$$

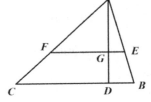

(A) $\sqrt{2}+1$ (B) $\sqrt{2}-1$ (C) 1   (D) $\sqrt{3}+1$ (E) $\sqrt{3}-1$

20. In isosceles trapezoid, $AB//DC$, $AD = BC$. $BE \perp DC$ at E. Find AB if $BE = AB$, $DB = DC = 10$.

(A) 9   (B) 8   (C) 7   (D) 6   (E) 5

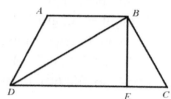

21. A square piece of paper 12 inches on each side is folded as shown, so that A falls on E, the midpoint of $\overline{DC}$. What is the number of square inches in the area of the triangular piece that extends beyond $\overline{FC}$ (the triangular piece is shaded in the diagram shown)?

(A) 8/3   (B) 9/4   (C) $1\frac{1}{2}$ (D) 7/4   (E) $\frac{\sqrt{5}}{2}$

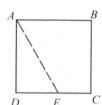
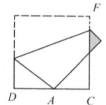

22. 1000 students are arranged in several rows (more than 16). The numbers of students in each row are consecutive positive integers. How many students are there in the first row?

(A) 20   (B) 25   (C) 28   (D) 44   (E) 80

23. In trapezoid $ABCD$, $AD =15$, $AB = 50$, and $BC = 20$. $DC - AB$ is a positive integer. What is the area of the trapezoid?

(A) 710   (B) 720   (C) 730   (D) 740   (E) 750.

95

24. Grouping all the even numbers {$2n$} by the rule: one number in group 1, two numbers in group 2, three numbers in group 3, 4 numbers in group 4, five numbers in group 5, and one number in group 6, two numbers in group 7, …, and so on. Groups 1 thg=rought 10 are shown as follows: (2), (4, 6), (8, 10, 12), (14, 16, 18, 20), (22, 24, 26, 28, 30); (32), (34, 36), (38, 40, 42), (44, 46, 48, 50), (52, 54, 56, 58, 60). If 2016 is the xth number in y group, what is the value of $x + y$?

(A) 320   (B) 325   (C) 339   (D) 344   (E) 345

25. As shown in the figure, $ABCD$ is a square with $AB = 16$. Triangle AEF is inscribed in $ABCD$. Find the area of the triangle EFC if $EF = 14$ and $\angle EAF = 45°$.

(A) 21   (B) 25   (C) 28   (D) 32   (E) 34

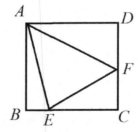

ANSWER KEYS:

1. E.
2. B.
3. C.
4. B.
5. E.
6. D.
7. C.
8. A.
9. E.
10. B.
11. A.
12. C.
13. D.
14. E
15. D.
16. C.
17. E.
18. C.
19. A.
20. D.
21. C.
22. C.
23. E.
24. C.
25. D.

SOLUTIONS:

1. E.

The scouts bought $2015/65 = 31$ groups of 65 candy bars at a total cost of $31 \times 31 = 961$ dollars. They sold $2015/13 = 155$ groups of thirteen candy bars for a total of 155×10 1550 dollars. Their profit was $\$1550 - \$961 = \$589$.

2. B.

We have $\dfrac{x}{100} \times x = 729$ $\Rightarrow$ $x^2 = 72900$ $\Rightarrow$ $x = \pm 270$

Since $x > 0$, it follows that $x = 270$.

3. C.

After the first day, $1 - \dfrac{2}{3} = \dfrac{1}{3}$ of the paint remains.

On the second day, $\dfrac{1}{3} \times \dfrac{2}{5} = \dfrac{2}{15}$ of the paint is used. So for the third day

$1 - \dfrac{2}{3} - \dfrac{2}{15} = \dfrac{15}{15} - \dfrac{10}{15} - \dfrac{2}{15} = \dfrac{3}{15} = \dfrac{1}{5}$ of the original gallon of paint is available.

4. B.

Let $3a$ be the width of the rectangle. Then the length is $4a$, and

$(3a)^2 + (4a)^2 = x^2$ $\Rightarrow$ $(5a)^2 = x^2$ $\Rightarrow$ $5a = x \Rightarrow$ $a = \dfrac{x}{5}$

The perimeter is $3a + 3a + 4a + 4a = 14a = 14 \times \dfrac{x}{5} = \dfrac{14}{5}x$.

5. E.

Counting from Alex anti-clock wisely, Cathy's number is 15. Counting from Cathy clock wisely, Bob's number is 7.

So counting from Alex anti-clock wisely, Bob's number will be $15 - 7 + 1 = 9$. So counting anti-clock wisely, there are $9 - 1 - 1 = 7$ people between Alex and Bob.

Counting from Alex clock wisely, Bob's number is 13. So there are $13 - 1 - 1 = 11$ people between Alex and Bob.

The total number of people will then be $7 + 11 + 1 + 1 = 20$.

6. D.

$$1000027 = 100^3 + 3^3 = (100 + 3)(10000 - 300 + 9) = 103 \times 9709$$
$$= 103 \times 7 \times 1387 = 103 \times 7 \times 19 \times 73.$$
The answer is $103 + 7 + 19 + 73 = 202$.

7. C.

An even sum requires either both dice are even or both dice are odd. The probability is

$$P = \frac{2}{6} \times \frac{4}{6} + \frac{4}{6} \times \frac{2}{6} = \frac{2}{9} + \frac{2}{9} = \frac{4}{9}.$$

8. A.

We see that $DF = DA - AF = DA - BC = 3 - 1 = 2$.
$DC = 3 + 1 = 4$.
Thus triangle DCF is a $30° - 60° - 90°$ right triangle.
The shaded area is the area of the trapezoid $ABCD$ – the areas of sectors ADE and ECB.
The answer is

$$\frac{(3+1) \times \sqrt{4^2 - 2^2}}{2} - \frac{\pi \times 3^2}{6} - \frac{\pi \times 1^2}{3}$$
$$= 4\sqrt{3} - \frac{11}{6}\pi.$$

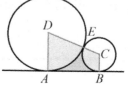 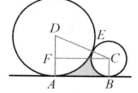

9. E.

The sequence begins 2017, 352, 160, 217, 352, 160, …

Thus after the initial term 2017, the sequence repeats the cycle 352, 160, 217.

Because $2015 = 671 \times 3 + 2 = 671 \times 3 + 1 + 1$, the 2015th term is the same as the first term of the repeating cycle, 352.

10. B.

Let $\overline{abcde} = x$. $\overline{abcde\,8} = 10x + 8$ and $\overline{2abcde} = 2 \times 10^5 + x$.

Then we have $\dfrac{10x + 8}{2} = 2 \times 10^5 + x$ $\qquad \Rightarrow \qquad 5x + 4 = 2 \times 10^5 + x$

$\Rightarrow \qquad 4x = 2 \times 10^5 - 4 \qquad \Rightarrow \qquad x = \dfrac{200000 - 4}{4} = 49999$.

The original six-digit number is 499998. The sum of the digits is $4 + 9 + 9 + 9 + 9 + 8 = 48$.

11. A.

There are total $2^{10} = 1024$ ways to flip ten coins.

The number of ways to get exactly 5 heads (HHHHHTTTTT) is : $\dfrac{10!}{5! \times 5!} = 252$.

The probability is $P = \dfrac{252}{1024} = \dfrac{63}{256}$.

12. C.

Method 1:

The following figure depicts car A and car B travelling toward each other at the same time.

We have $d = (r_A + r_B)t \qquad \Rightarrow \qquad d = (60 + 40) \times t$ $\qquad\qquad$ (1)

When car A starts 30 minutes, or 0.5 hours earlier, we have a different figure.

$$d = 60 \times x + (60 + 40) \times (t - 0.5) \tag{2}$$

Solving (1) and (2) we get:

$$60 \times x + (60 + 40) \times (t - 0.5) = (60 + 40) \times t \quad \Rightarrow \quad 60 \times x + 100t - 50 = 100t$$

$$\Rightarrow \quad x = \frac{50}{60} \text{ hours} = 50 \text{ minutes.}$$

Method 2:

Since the two cars would meet 30 minutes (0.5 hours) earlier if car A started traveling x minutes earlier, in this 30 minutes interval, car A would have traveled $60 \times 0.5 = 30$ km and car B would have traveled $40 \times 0.5 = 20$ km. So car A actually covered 50 km in one hour (30 minutes + 30 minutes). Therefore car A starts $50/60 = 50$ minutes earlier.

13. D.

There are $\binom{10}{3} = 120$ ways to choose three bills.

A sum of at least \$50 is obtained by

(1) choosing two \$30 bills and one of the eight smaller bills (1, 1, 5, 5, 10, 10, 20, 20): $\binom{2}{2}\binom{8}{1} = 8$

(2) choosing one \$30 bill and two \$20 or two \$10 bills: $\binom{2}{1}\binom{2}{2} + \binom{2}{1}\binom{2}{2} = 4$.

(3) choosing one \$30 bill, one \$20 bill, and one of the six smaller bills (1, 1, 5, 5, 10, 10): $\binom{2}{1}\binom{2}{1}\binom{6}{1} = 24$.

(4) choosing two \$20 bills and one of the two smaller bills (10, 10): $\binom{2}{2}\binom{2}{1} = 4$

Hence the probability is $P = \dfrac{8+4+24+4}{120} = \dfrac{40}{120} = \dfrac{1}{3}$.

14. (E).
The condition is equivalent to $128n^2 > n^3 > 2^6 = 64$, so $128n^2 > n^3$ and $n^3 > 64$

This implies that $128 > n > 4$. So n can be any of the $127 - 5 + 1 = 123$ integers strictly.

15. D.
$$2^4 \times 3^6 \times 5^{10} \times 7^9 = (2^3 \times 3^6 \times 5^9 \times 7^9) \times 2^1 \times 5^1 = (2^1 \times 3^2 \times 5^3 \times 7^3)^3 \times 2^1 \times 5^1$$

Any factor of $2^1 \times 3^2 \times 5^3 \times 7^3$ will be a positive cube.

The number of factors of $N = 2^1 \times 3^2 \times 5^3 \times 7^3$ can be calculated as $d(N) = (1 + 1)(2 + 1)(3 + 1)(3 + 1) = 2 \times 3 \times 4 \times 4 = 96$.

Hence there are 96 distinct cubes that divide $2^4 \times 3^6 \times 5^{10} \times 7^9$.

16. C.
Let $100a + 10b + c$ be the three-digit number. When $a + b$ is subtracted the result is $9(11a + b)$. Since the last digit is 7, $(11a + b)$ must end in 3.

Case 1: $11a + b = 3$. No solutions.

Case 2: $11a + b = 13$.
$a = 1$ and $b = 2$.   We have 10 such numbers: 120, 121, ..., 129.

Case 3: $11a + b = 23$.
$a = 2$ and $b = 1$.   We have 10 such numbers: 210, 211, ..., 219.

Case 4: $11a + b = 33$.
$a = 3$ and $b = 0$.   We have 10 such numbers: 300, 301, ..., 309.

Case 5: $11a + b = 43$. No solutions.

Case 6: $11a + b = 53$.
$a = 4$ and $b = 9$.   We have 10 such numbers: 490, 491, ..., 499.

Case 7: $11a + b = 63$.
$a = 5$ and $b = 4$.
The number is bigger than 500.
We stop here and the answer is $10 + 10 + 10 + 10 = 40$.

17. E.

Since $1 + 2 + \cdots + n = \dfrac{n(n+1)}{2}$, $\dfrac{n!}{\dfrac{n(n+1)}{2}} = \dfrac{2n(n-1)!}{n(n+1)} = \dfrac{2(n-1)!}{(n+1)}$.

We see that $n!$ is divisible by $1 + 2 + \ldots + n$ if $n + 1$ is not an odd prime. There are 24 odd prime numbers less than 100, so we must subtract these 24 from the initial 100 n possible values. When $n = 100$, $n + 1 = 101$, which is an odd prime, so we must also subtract this n value. Therefore, there are $100 - 24 - 1 = 75$ positive integers.

18. C.
The two sequences can be expressed as

$$a_n = 1 + (n-1) \times 6$$

$$b_m = 4 + (m-1) \times 7$$

$$2015 = 1 + (n-1) \times 6$$

$$n = \left\lfloor \frac{2015-1}{6} + 1 \right\rfloor = 336.$$ The greatest value for n is 336.

$$2015 = 4 + (m-1) \times 7.$$

$$m = \left\lfloor \frac{2015-4}{7} + 1 \right\rfloor = 288.$$ The greatest value for m is 288.

We want to find the number of common terms so we set $a_n = b_m$

$1 + (n-1) \times 6 = 4 + (m-1) \times 7$ or $7m + 2 = 6n$

Solve for m, $7m + 2 = 0 \pmod 6$ $\Rightarrow$ $m = 4 \pmod 6$

m can then be 4, 10, 16, …

Calculate the number of m's: $288 = 4 + (k-1) \times 6$

so $k = \left\lfloor \frac{288-4}{6} + 1 \right\rfloor = 48.$

19. A.

$$\frac{S_{\triangle ABC}}{S_{\triangle AEF}} = \left(\frac{AD}{AG} \right)^2 \quad \Rightarrow \quad 2 = \left(\frac{AG+GD}{AG} \right)^2 \quad \Rightarrow \quad \frac{AG+GD}{AG} = \sqrt{2}$$

$$\Rightarrow \quad 1 + \frac{GD}{AG} = \sqrt{2} \quad \Rightarrow \quad \frac{GD}{AG} = \sqrt{2} - 1 \Rightarrow$$

$$\frac{AG}{GD} = \frac{1}{\sqrt{2}-1} = \sqrt{2} + 1.$$

20. D.

Method 1:

Connect AC and draw $BM//AC$ to meet DC at M.

Since $AB//DC$ and $BM//AC$, $AB = CM$, AC

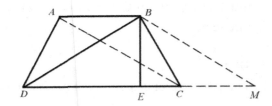

$= BM.$

Since $AD = BC$, $BD = AC$. Thus $BM = BD = 10$.

Since $BE \perp DC$, $DE = EM$.

We know that $DC = 10$. Let $DE = x$.

It follows that $CE = 10 - x$ and $EM = x$, so $CM = EM - CE = 2x - 10$.

Since $BE = AB = CM$, $BE = 2x - 10$.

By the Pythagorean Theorem, we have $BE^2 + DE^2 = BD^2$, or

$(2x - 10)^2 + x^2 = 100$.

This can be simplified into $5x^2 - 40x = 0$.

Since $x > 0$, $x = 8$.

Therefore $AB = 2x - 10 = 6$.

Method 2:

We know that $10^2 = BC^2 + AB \times 10$ (1)

Draw $AF \perp DC$ at E. We know that

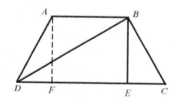

$$BC^2 = BE^2 + EC^2 = AB^2 + \left(\frac{DC - AB}{2}\right)^2 = AB^2 + \left(\frac{10 - AB}{2}\right)^2 \qquad (2)$$

Substituting (2) into (1), we get:

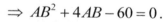

$$10^2 = AB^2 + \left(\frac{10 - AB}{2}\right)^2 + AB \times 10 \quad \Rightarrow$$

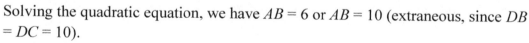

$$10^2 = AB^2 + \left(\frac{10 - AB}{2}\right)^2 + AB \times 10$$

$\Rightarrow AB^2 + 4AB - 60 = 0$.

Solving the quadratic equation, we have $AB = 6$ or $AB = 10$ (extraneous, since $DB = DC = 10$).

Therefore $AB = 6$.

21. C.

Applying Pythagorean Theorem to $\triangle ADG$: $6^2 + (12-x)^2 = x^2$ $\Rightarrow$ $x = 15/2$.

So the area of $\triangle ADG$ is:

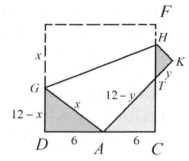

$$S_{\triangle ADG} = \frac{6(12-x)}{2} = \frac{6(12-\dfrac{15}{2})}{2} = \frac{27}{2}.$$

We see that $\triangle ADG \sim \triangle TCA \sim \triangle KH$.

So we have $\dfrac{AG}{AT} = \dfrac{GD}{AC}$ $\Rightarrow$ $\dfrac{x}{12-y} = \dfrac{12-x}{6}$ $\Rightarrow$

$$\frac{\dfrac{15}{2}}{12-y} = \frac{12-\dfrac{15}{2}}{6} \Rightarrow y = 2.$$

We know that $\dfrac{S_{\triangle HKT}}{S_{\triangle ADG}} = (\dfrac{KT}{AD})^2 = (\dfrac{2}{6})^2$ $\Rightarrow$

$$S_{\triangle HKT} = (\frac{2}{6})^2 S_{\triangle ADG} = \frac{\dfrac{27}{2}}{9} = \frac{27}{18} = \frac{3}{2} = 1\frac{1}{2}.$$

22. C.

Let m be the number of students in the first row.

$m + (m+1) + (m+2) + ... + (m+k-1) = 1000$

$(2m + k - 1) \times k = 1000 \times 2 = 2^4 \times 5^3$.

We know that $k > 16$, and $2m + k - 1$ and k must have different parity, so we can only have $(2m + k - 1) \times k = 1000 \times 2 = 2^4 \times 5^3 = 25 \times 80$

So $k = 25$ and $2m + k - 1 = 80$ $\Rightarrow$ $m = 28$.

23. E.

Let E and F be the feet of the perpendiculars from A and B to DC.

In right $\triangle AED$, $15^2 - DE^2 = x^2 \Rightarrow$ $15^2 - y^2 = x^2$ (1)

In right $\triangle BFC$, $20^2 - FC^2 = x^2$ $\Rightarrow$ $20^2 - z^2 = x^2$ (2)

From (1) and (2) we get: $15^2 - y^2 = 20^2 - z^2$

$z^2 - y^2 = 20^2 - 15^2 \Rightarrow (z-y)(z+y) = 175 = 1 \times 175 = 5 \times 35 = 7 \times 25$ (3)

We see that $DC - AB = z + y$ is an integer. So $(z - y)$ must also be an integer.

From (3), we get

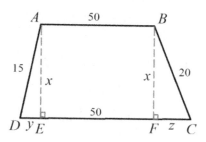

$\left.\begin{array}{l} z - y = 1 \\ z + y = 175 \end{array}\right\}$

$\left.\begin{array}{l} z - y = 5 \\ z + y = 35 \end{array}\right\}$

$\left.\begin{array}{l} z - y = 7 \\ z + y = 25 \end{array}\right\}$

Only the last system of equations give the correct solutions with $y = 9$ and $z = 16$. Substituting $y = 9$ into (1): $x = 12$.

$DC = DE + EF + FC = 9 + 50 + 16 = 75$. Then the area of trapezoid is $(AB + DC)$ $\cdot AE / 2 = (50 + 75) \cdot 12/2 = 125 \cdot 6 = 750$.

24. C.

We batch the numbers as follows:

Group 1: (2), (4, 6), (8, 10, 12), …, (22, 24, 26, 28, 30);

Group 2: (32), (34, 36), (38, 40, 42), …, (52, 54, 56, 58, 60);

Group 3: (62), (64, 66), (68, 70, 72),…, (82, 84, 86, 88, 90);

………………………

We see that each batch has 15 even numbers.

2016 is 1008th number in $\{2n\}$.

$1008 = 67 \times 15 + 3$.

Since each batch has 5 groups, $67 \times 5 = 335$.

The three numbers follow: group 336: (2012), group 337: (2014, 2016).

Thus 2016 is the second number in the group 337 group. The answer is $2 + 337 = 339$.

25. D.

Extend EB to G such that $BG = DF$. Connect AG.

Since $AB = AD$, $\triangle ABG \cong \triangle ADF$. Thus $\angle 2 = \angle 3$.

Since $\angle AEF = = 45°$, $\angle 1 + \angle 2 = = 45°$. Therefore $\angle 1 + \angle 3$
$= 45°$.

In $\triangle AEF$ and $\triangle AEG$, $AE = AE$, $AF = AG$, $\angle EAF = \angle EAG$. Therefore $\triangle AEF$
$\cong \triangle AEG$. $EF = EG = 14$.

$$S_{\triangle EFC} = S_{ABCD} - S_{ABEFD} = S_{ABCD} - 2S_{AEG} = 16^2 - 2 \times \frac{1}{2} \times 14 \times 16 = 32.$$

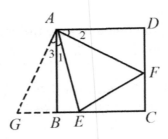

American Mathematics Competitions

Practice 7
AMC 10

(American Mathematics Contest 10)

INSTRUCTIONS

1. This is a twenty-five question multiple choice test. Each question is followed by answers marked A, B, C, D and E. Only one of these is correct.

2. You will have 75 minutes to complete the test.

3. No aids are permitted other than scratch paper, graph paper, rulers, and erasers. No problems on the test will require the use of a calculator.

4. Figures are not necessarily drawn to scale.

5. SCORING: You will receive 6 points for each correct answer, 1.5 points for each problem left unanswered, and 0 points for each incorrect answer.

1. Three sandwiches and two sodas cost $10.5 at John's Fast Food. Two sandwiches and three sodas cost $9.5 at John's Fast Food. How many dollars will it cost to purchase 1 sandwich and 1 soda?

(A) $2   (B) $3   (C) $4   (D) $5   (E) $2.5

2. The ratio of Alice's age to Betsy's age is 5 : 7 now. Alice was 20 years old five years ago. What will be the ratio of Alice's age to Betsy's age in five years?

(A) 5/7   (B) 3/4   (C) 4/7   (D) 3/7   (E) 7/9

3. A rectangle $ABCD$ with the length $AB = 15$ cm and width $BC = 11$ cm is cut into two parts along the dashed line as shown in the figure. $AE = 4$ cm and $CF = 5$ cm. What is the sum of the perimeters of the two parts?

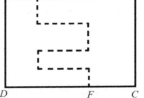

(A) 26 cm   (B) 30 cm   (C) 41 cm
(D) 100 cm   (E) 110 cm

4. What is $2^{10} - 2^1 - 2^2 - 2^3 - 2^4 - 2^5 - 2^6 - 2^7 - 2^8 - 2^9$?

(A) 2   (B) 1022   (C) 0   (D) 6   (E) 4

5. Alex's class has less than forty students. One afternoon after class, two-seventh of the students went to a football game, one-five of the students went to a baseball game, and the rest of the students went to a writing contest. How many students went to the writing contest?

(A) 10   (B) 14   (C) 18   (D) 20   (E) 24

6. Circles of diameter 6 inch and 12 inches have the same center. The smaller circle is painted yellow, and the portion outside the smaller circle and inside the larger circle is painted white. What is the ratio of the white-painted area to the yellow-painted area?

(A) 2   (B) 3   (C) 6   (D) 8   (E) 9

7. During Thanksgiving, a store uses the following discounts for an electrical appliance originally marked $100:
      (1) Take $20 off the original price and then deduct 20%.
      (2) Discount by 20% of the original price, and then take $20 off.
 What is the positive difference of money a customer can have from these two ways?

(A) $0   (B) $1   (C) $2   (D) $3   (E) $4

8. A 3×3 square, 3×5 rectangle, and a 5×7 rectangle are contained within a large square without overlapping at any interior point, and the sides of the square are parallel to the sides of the three given figures. What is the smallest possible area of the large square?

(A) 16   (B) 25   (C) 36   (D) 49   (E) 64

9. A square is inscribed in a semicircle as shown. If the area of the shaded regions is $10\pi - 16$, find the side length of the square.

(A) 4   (B) 5   (C) $2\sqrt{2}$ (D) π (E) 3

10. The list 1, 3, 9, 25, 69, 189, 517, … has the following property: starting from the third number in the list, each number is 1 more than 2 times the sum the two numbers before it. For example, $9 = 1 + 2 \times (1 + 3)$. What is the remainder when the 2015th number in the list is divided by 6?

(A) 0   (B) 1   (C) 2   (D) 3   (E) 4

11. Write the number 100 as the sum of two numbers, where one of the two is divisible by 7 and the other one divisible by 11. What is the smaller number?

(A) 14   (B) 22   (C) 56   (D) 44   (E) 64

12. Find m^3 if $m^2 = 5 + 2\sqrt{6}$.

(A) $9\sqrt{3} + 11\sqrt{2}$ or $11\sqrt{2} - 9\sqrt{3}$ (B) $9\sqrt{3} - 11\sqrt{2}$ or $11\sqrt{2} + 9\sqrt{3}$

(C) $9\sqrt{3} - 11\sqrt{2}$ or $11\sqrt{2} - 9\sqrt{3}$ (D) $9\sqrt{3} + 11\sqrt{2}$ or $-11\sqrt{2} - 9\sqrt{3}$

(E) $9\sqrt{2} + 11\sqrt{3}$ or $-11\sqrt{3} - 9\sqrt{2}$

13. The sum of 15 consecutive positive integers is a perfect square. Find the smallest possible value of this sum.

(A) 125   (B) 185   (C) 225   (D) 245   (E) 255

14. What is the last three digits in the sum $1! + 2! + 3! + 4! + 5! + 6! + 7! + 8! + 9! + 10! + 13! + 14! + 15! + \cdots + 2015!$?

(A) 713   (B) 813   (C) 913   (D) 610   (E) 900

15. A circle of radius 6 is tangent to a circle of radius 2. The sides of $\triangle ABC$ are tangent to the circles as shown, and the sides AB and AC are congruent. What is the area of the shaded regions?

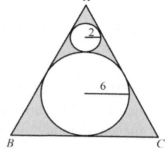

(A) $108\sqrt{3} - 40\pi$ (B) $108\sqrt{3} - 36\pi$

(C) $108\sqrt{2} - 40\pi$ (D) $108\sqrt{2} - 4\pi$ (E) $108\sqrt{3}$

16. If $x^2 - \dfrac{1}{x^2} = 2$, then what is the value of $x^4 + \dfrac{1}{x^4}$?

(A) 1   (B) 3   (C) 6   (D) 9   (E) 10

17. Two swimmers, at opposite ends of a 50-meter pool, start to swim the length of the pool, one at the rate of 3 meters per second, the other at 2 meters per second. They swim back and forth for 2 minutes. Allowing no loss of time at the turns, find the numbers of times they pass each other.

(A) 2   (B) 4   (C) 6   (D) 8   (E) 10

18. Leap Day, February 29, 2012, occurred on a Wednesday . On what day of the week will Leap Day, February 29, 2028, occur?

(A) Tuesday (B) Wednesday (C) Thursday (D) Friday (E) Saturday

19. Emma and Kyle take turns rolling a 6-sided die. Emma rolls first. What is the probability that Emma is the first person to roll a 5?

(A) 5/11   (B) 6/11   (C) 7/11   (D) 8/11   (E) 4/11

20. How many different ways can seven students be seated in a row of seven seats if there must be exactly two people between Alex and Betsy?

(A) 720   (B) 840   (C) 960   (D) 980   (E) 982

21. Three distinct positive integers are randomly chosen between 1 and 20, inclusive. What is the probability that the sum of the three distinct positive integers is a multiple of 6?

(A) 190/441   (B) 150/1711   (C) 16/95   (D) 59/300   (E) 49/380.

22. A triangle is partitioned into three triangles and a quadrilateral by drawing two lines from vertices to their opposite sides. The areas of the three triangles are 10, 20, and 16, as shown. What is the area of the shaded quadrilateral?

(A) 24   (B) 28   (C) 32   (D) 36   (E) 44

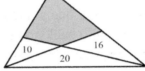

23. In rectangle *ABCD, E* is the midpoint of *AD, F* is the midpoint of *CE.* What is the area of the rectangle *ABCD* if the area of triangle *BDF* is 252 cm^2?

(A) 2014   (B) 2015 (C) 2016   (D) 2017   (E) 2018

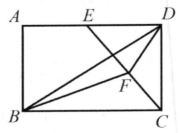

24. An octahedron is formed by joining the centers of adjoining faces of a 10 cm × 15 cm × 20 cm rectangular prism. What is the volume of this octahedron?

(A) 200   (B) 300   (C) 400   (D) 500   (E) 550

25. If the number 11111 in base b is a square number, what is the value of b?

(A) 2   (B) 3   (C) 6   (D) 9   (E) 11

ANSWER KEYS

1. C.
2. B.
3. E.
4. A.
5. C.
6. B.
7. E.
8. E.
9. A.
10. D.
11. D.
12. D.
13. C.
14. C.
15. A.
16. C.
17. C.
18. A.
19. B.
20. C.
21. C.
22. E.
23. C.
24. D.
25. B.

SOLUTIONS:

1. C.

Let x be the cost of each sandwich and y be the cost of each soda.

$3x + 2y = 10.5$ (1)

$2x + 3y = 9.5$ (2)

$(1) + (2): 5(x + y) = 20$ $\Rightarrow$ $x + y = \$4.$

2. B.

Alice is $20 + 5 = 25$ years old now. Betsy's age is $\frac{7}{5} \times 25 = 35$ years old.

In 5 years, Alice will be $25 + 5 = 30$ years old. Betsy will be $35 + 5 = 40$ years old. The ratio will be $30/40 = 3/4$.

3. E.

The sum of the perimeters of the two parts = the perimeters of the original rectangle + 2 × the length of the dashed line

$= 2(15 + 11) + 2[11 + (15 - 4 - 5) \times 3] = 52 + 58 = 110$ cm.

4. A.

$2^{10} - 2^9 - 2^8 - 2^7 - 2^6 - 2^5 - 2^4 - 2^3 - 2^2 - 2^1$

$= 2^9 (2 - 1) - 2^8 - 2^7 - 2^6 - 2^5 - 2^4 - 2^3 - 2^2 - 2^1$

$= 2^8 (2 - 1) - 2^7 - 2^6 - 2^5 - 2^4 - 2^3 - 2^2 - 2^1$

. . . .

$= 2^3 (2 - 1) - 2^2 - 2^1$

$= 2^2 (2 - 1) - 2^1 = 2.$

5. C.

The number of students in the class should be a multiple of 7 and 5, which must be 35.

So $35 - (2/7 + 1/5) \times 35 = 18$.

6. B.

The circle with diameter 6 has area $\pi(\frac{6}{2})^2 = 9\pi$.

The circle with diameter 12 has $\pi(\frac{12}{2})^2 = 36\pi$

Therefore the ratio of the yellow-painted area to the white-painted area is $\frac{(36-9)\pi}{9\pi} = \frac{27}{9} = 3$.

7. E.

The first way: $(100 - 20) \times 0.8 = \$64$

The second way: $100 \times 0.8 - 20 = \$60$.

$64 - 60 = \$4$.

8. E.

The side length of the square is at least equal to the sum of the smaller

dimensions of the rectangles, which is $5 + 3 = 8$. The small square can fit in as shown. Thus the area if $8^2 = 64$.

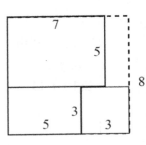

9. A.

Let a be the side length of the square, and r be the radius of the semicircle. We have

$$\frac{\pi r^2}{2} - a^2 = 10\pi - 16 \qquad\qquad (1)$$

By Pythagorean Theorem, we have

$$r^2 = a^2 + (\frac{1}{2}a)^2 \qquad \Rightarrow \qquad r^2 = \frac{5}{4}a^2 \qquad\qquad (2)$$

Substituting (2) into (2):

$$\frac{\pi}{2}(\frac{5a^2}{4}) - a^2 = 10\pi - 16 \qquad \Rightarrow \qquad a^2(\frac{5\pi}{8} - 1) = 10\pi - 16$$

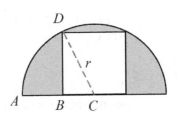

$$\Rightarrow \qquad a^2(\frac{5\pi-8}{8}) = 2(5\pi-8) \qquad \Rightarrow \qquad a^2 = 16 \qquad \Rightarrow \qquad a = 4.$$

10. D.

Note the pattern of the remainders when these numbers are divided by 6: 1, 3, 3, 1, 3, 3, 1, 3, 3, ...

Since $2015 \div 3 = 671\ r\ 2$, the remainder is 3.

11. D.

$7x + 11y = 100 \qquad \Rightarrow \qquad 7x = 100 - 11y$

$100 - 11y \equiv 0\ (\text{mod } 7) \Rightarrow \qquad 9 - 4y \equiv 0\ (\text{mod } 7) \qquad \Rightarrow \qquad 16 - 4y \equiv 0\ (\text{mod } 7)$

$y = 4$; $x = 8$. The smaller number is 44.

12. D.

Since $m^2 = 5 + 2\sqrt{6}$, $m = \pm(\sqrt{3} + \sqrt{2})$.

$m^3 = m \times m^2 = \pm(\sqrt{3} + \sqrt{2}) \times (5 + 2\sqrt{6})$

$= \pm(9\sqrt{3} + 11\sqrt{2})$.

13. C.

$N = m + (m+1) + (m+2) + (m+3) + ... + (m+k-1)$

$= \dfrac{(m+m+k-1)k}{2} = \dfrac{(2m+k-1)k}{2}$

$= \dfrac{(2m+14)15}{2} = 15m + 105 = 15(m+7)$

Since we want the smallest sum, we let $m = 8$.

The answer is 225.

14. C.

Since $\left\lfloor \dfrac{15!}{5} \right\rfloor = 3$, 15! contains the factor 1000. Thus whenever $n \geq 15$, it suffices to determine the last three digits of 1! + 2! + 3! + 4! + 5! + 6 ! + 7! + 8! + 9! + 10! + 13! + 14!.

We see that 13! + 14! = 13! (1 + 14) = 13! × 5 × 3. So we have three 5's as the factor of 13! × 5 × 3. Thus the last three digits of 13! + 14! is 000.

8! + 9! + 10! = 8!(1 + 9 + 9 × 10) = 8! × 100. So the last three digits of 8! + 9! + 10! is also 000.

So we have 1! + 2! + 3! + 4! + 5! + 6 ! + 7! to examine.

1 + 2 + 6 + 24 + 120 + 720 + 5040 = 5913.

So the answer is 913.

15. A.

Draw $AH \perp BC$ and meets BC at H. Let F and G denote the centers of the smaller and larger circles, respectively. Let E and D be the points on AC that are also on the smaller and larger circles, respectively.

Since $\triangle AEF$, $\triangle ADG$ and $\triangle AHC$ are similar right triangles, we have

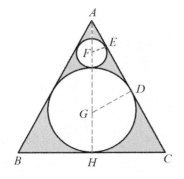

$$\frac{AF}{AG} = \frac{FE}{GD} \quad \Rightarrow \quad \frac{AG - FG}{AG} = \frac{FE}{GD} \quad \Rightarrow$$

$$1 - \frac{2+6}{AG} = \frac{2}{6} \quad \Rightarrow \quad \frac{8}{AG} = \frac{2}{3} \Rightarrow \quad AG = 12$$

$\triangle AEF$, $\triangle ADG$ and $\triangle AHC$ are all $30° - 60° - 90°$ right triangles.

$\triangle ABC$ is an equilateral triangle with altitude $AH = 18$.

The area of is $\triangle ABC$ $\frac{\sqrt{3}}{4}(AB)^2 = \frac{\sqrt{3}}{4}(\frac{2}{\sqrt{3}} AH)^2 = \frac{\sqrt{3}}{4} \times \frac{4}{3} \times 18^2 = 108\sqrt{3}$.

The area of the shaded regions is $108\sqrt{3} - \pi \times (2)^2 - \pi \times (6)^2 = 108\sqrt{3} - 40\pi$

16. C.

We know that $x^2 - \dfrac{1}{x^2} = 2$. So $x^4 - 1 = 2x^2$ $\Rightarrow$ $x^4 - 2x^2 = 1$

(1)

We also know that $\dfrac{1}{x^2} = x^2 - 2$ $\Rightarrow$ $\dfrac{1}{x^4} = (x^2 - 2)^2$

(2)

Thus $x^4 + \dfrac{1}{x^4} = x^4 + (x^2 - 2)^2 = x^4 + x^4 - 4x^2 + 4 = 2(x^4 - 2x^2 + 2) = 2(1+2) = 6$

17. C.

As shown in the figure, it takes A t seconds to get back to the ends where he began at the relative speed (3 + 2):

$(3 + 2)t = 50 \times 2 = 100$ $\Rightarrow$ $t = 20$ seconds.

Thus, every 20 seconds they will meet once.

In 2 minutes, or $2 \times 60 = 120$ seconds, they will meet $120 \div 20 = 6$ times.

18. A.

In the years from 2012 through 2028, Each Leap Day occurs $3 \times 365 + 366 = 1461$ days after the preceding Leap Day. When 1461 is divided by 7 the remainder is 5. So the day of the week advances 5 days for each 4-year cycle. In the four cycles from 2012 to 2028, the Leap Day will advance 20 days. So Leap Day in 2028 will occur one day of the week earlier than in 2012, that is, on a Tuesday.

19. B.

Case 1: Emma rolls a 5 in the first roll.
The probability is 1/6.

Case 2: Emma rolls a 5 in the third roll.
The probability is (5/6)(5/6)(1/6).

Case 3: Emma rolls a 5 in the fifth roll.
The probability is $(5/6)(5/6)(5/6)(5/6)(1/6)$.

We see the pattern that the probability can be expressed as:

$$P = \frac{1}{6} + (\frac{5}{6})^2 \times \frac{1}{6} + (\frac{5}{6})^4 \times \frac{1}{6} + \cdots$$

This is an infinite geometric sequence with common ratio $(\frac{5}{6})^2$ and first term $\frac{1}{6}$.

So $P = \dfrac{\frac{1}{6}}{1 - (\frac{5}{6})^2} = \dfrac{\frac{1}{6}}{\frac{11}{36}} = \dfrac{6}{11}$.

20. C.

We have $\binom{5}{2}$ ways to select C and D between Alex and Betsy. We let Alex, C, D, and Betsy be one unit. The number of arrangements will be 4!

| Alex $\mid C \mid D \mid$ Betsy | S_5 | S_6 | S_7 |

Alex and Betsy can switch their positions and C and D can switch their positions as well. So the answer will be $\binom{5}{2} \times 4! \times 2 \times 2 = 960$.

21. C.
Place each of the integers in a pile based on the remainder when the integer is divided by 6.

Remainder	The integers	Total
0	6, 12, 18,	3
1	1, 7, 13, 19	4
2	2, 8, 14, 20,	4
3	3, 9, 15,	3
4	4, 10, 16,	3
5	5, 11, 17,	3

We see that

$5 + 4 + 3 = 6 \times 2,$ $5 + 1 + 0 = 6 \times 1,$ $4 + 2 + 0 = 6 \times 1,$ $3 + 2 + 1 = 6 \times 1,$

$5 + 5 + 2 = 6 \times 2,$ $4 + 1 + 1 = 6 \times 1,$ $0 + 0 + 0 = 6 \times 0,$ $2 + 2 + 2 = 6 \times 1,$

$4 + 4 + 4 = 6 \times 2,$ $3 + 3 + 0 = 6 \times 1,$

The probability is

$$P = \frac{3 \cdot 3 \cdot 3 + 3 \cdot 4 \cdot 3 + 3 \cdot 4 \cdot 3 + 3 \cdot 4 \cdot 4 + \binom{3}{2}\binom{4}{1} + \binom{3}{1}\binom{4}{2} + \binom{3}{3} + \binom{4}{3} + \binom{3}{3} + \binom{3}{2} \cdot 3}{\binom{20}{3}}$$

$$= \frac{27 + 36 + 36 + 48 + 12 + 18 + 1 + 4 + 1 + 9}{\dfrac{20 \times 19 \times 18}{6}} = \frac{192}{1140} = \frac{16}{95}.$$

22. E.

Connect AF.

$$\frac{S_{\triangle ABF}}{S_{\triangle BFC}} = \frac{S_{\triangle AFD}}{S_{\triangle FDC}} \qquad \Rightarrow \qquad \frac{10 + x}{20} = \frac{y}{16}$$

Similarly, we have $\dfrac{S_{\triangle ACF}}{S_{\triangle BCF}} = \dfrac{S_{\triangle AEF}}{S_{\triangle EFB}} \qquad \Rightarrow \qquad \dfrac{16 + y}{20} = \dfrac{x}{10}$

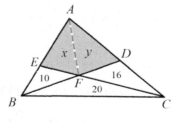

Solving the equations for x and y, we get $x = 20$, and $y = 24$. The area of $AEFD$ is 44.

23. C.

Connect BE. Let x be the area of rectangle $ABCD$.

$$S_{\triangle BEC} = \frac{x}{2} \text{ and } S_{\triangle EDC} = \frac{x}{4}.$$

Since $EF = FC$, $S_{\triangle BCF} = \frac{1}{2} S_{\triangle BEC} = \frac{1}{2} \times \frac{x}{2} = \frac{x}{4}.$

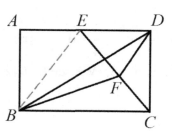

and $S_{\triangle CDF} = \dfrac{1}{2}S_{\triangle EDC} = \dfrac{1}{2} \times \dfrac{x}{4} = \dfrac{x}{8}$.

Thus $S_{BCDF} = \dfrac{x}{4} + \dfrac{x}{8} = \dfrac{3x}{8}$.

We also know that $S_{\triangle BCD} = \dfrac{x}{2}$.

So $S_{\triangle BDF} = \dfrac{x}{2} - \dfrac{3x}{8} = \dfrac{x}{8}$ $\Rightarrow$ $\dfrac{x}{8} = 252$ $\Rightarrow$ $x = 252 \times 8 = 2016$.

24. D.

P, Q, R, S, V, V' are the center of faces $ABCD, ABB'A',$ $A'B'C'D', CC'D'D, ADD'A', BCC'B'$, respectively.

Let $AB = a$, $BC = b$, and $BB' = c$.

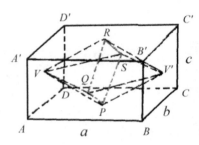

Since the plane $PQRS \perp VV'$, its area is $\dfrac{1}{2}bc$.

We know that $VV' = a$, The volume of the octahedron is

$\dfrac{1}{3} \times (\dfrac{1}{2}bc) \times a = \dfrac{1}{6}abc = \dfrac{1}{6} \times 10 \times 15 \times 20 = 500$.

25. B.

We write 11111 as $11111 = b^4 + b^3 + b^2 + b + 1$.

We know that $(b^2 + \dfrac{b}{2})^2 < b^4 + b^3 + b^2 + b + 1 < (b^2 + \dfrac{b}{2} + 1)^2$.

If $11111 = b^4 + b^3 + b^2 + b + 1$ is a square number, we must have

$(b^2 + \dfrac{b}{2} + \dfrac{1}{2})^2 = b^4 + b^3 + b^2 + b + 1$,

or $\dfrac{b^2}{4} - \dfrac{b}{2} - \dfrac{3}{4} = 0$ $\Rightarrow$ $(b-3)(b+1) = 0$.

Thus $b = 3$. We see that $11111 = 102^2$.

American Mathematics Competitions

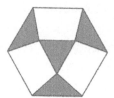

Practice 8
AMC 10

(American Mathematics Contest 10)

INSTRUCTIONS

1. This is a twenty-five question multiple choice test. Each question is followed by answers marked A, B, C, D and E. Only one of these is correct.

2. You will have 75 minutes to complete the test.

3. No aids are permitted other than scratch paper, graph paper, rulers, and erasers. No problems on the test will require the use of a calculator.

4. Figures are not necessarily drawn to scale.

5. SCORING: You will receive 6 points for each correct answer, 1.5 points for each problem left unanswered, and 0 points for each incorrect answer.

1. One ticket to a show costs $30 at full price. Kathy buys 8 tickets using a coupon that gives her a 15% discount. Pat buys 8 tickets using a coupon that gives her a 35% discount. How many more dollars does Kathy pay than Pat?

(A) 28   (B) 38   (C) 48   (D) 58   (E) 68

2. A water tank has a rectangular base that measures 200 cm by 60 cm and has a height of 70 cm. It is filled with water to a height of 50 cm. A stone with a rectangular base that measures 60 cm by 30 cm and a height of 20 cm is placed in the tank. By how many centimeters does the water rise?

(A) 1   (B) 2   (C) 3   (D) 4   (E) 4.5

3. The largest of three consecutive odd integers is five times the smallest. What is their sum?

(A) 4   (B) 6   (C) 8   (D) 9   (E) 10

4. In a jar of red, green, and blue marbles, all but 12 are red marbles, all but 16 are green, and all but 8 are blue. How many marbles are in the jar?

(A) 12   (B) 16   (C) 18   (D) 20   (E) 36

5. The Don family consists of a mother, a father, and some children. The average age of the members of the family is 17, the mother is 35 years old, and the average age of the father and children is 14. How many children are in the family?

(A) 2   (B) 3   (C) 4   (D) 5   (E) 6

6. The numbers from 3 to 10 are placed at the vertices of a cube in such a manner that the sum of the four numbers on each face is the same. What is this common sum?

(A) 24   (B) 26   (C) 28   (D) 30   (E) 34

7. Jake's age is X years, which is also the sum of the ages of his three children. His age Y years ago was three times the sum of their ages then. What is X/Y?

A. 2   B. 3   C. 3/2   D. 4/3   E. 4.

8. A triangle with side lengths in the ratio $5 : 12 : 13$ is inscribed in a circle of radius 26.
What is the area of the triangle?

(A) 960   (B) 480   (C) 160π (D) 950   (E) 488

9. Two distinct integers are chosen at random from 0 to 9, inclusive. What is the probability that the sum is greater than 14?

(A) $\dfrac{16}{45}$ (B) $\dfrac{8}{15}$ (C) $\dfrac{7}{45}$ (D) $\dfrac{4}{45}$ (E) $\dfrac{2}{45}$

10. Consider the two squares $ABCD$ and $EFGB$ with side lengths of 6 and 10, respectively, next to each other as shown. One quarter circle of radius of 10 is drawn inside the square $ABCD$ with the center B. Connect AF and CF. Find the area of the shaded region.

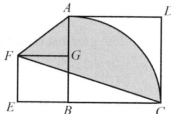

(A) $45\sqrt{3}$ (B) $45\sqrt{2}$ (C) 25π (D) 20π (E) 36

11. A bag contains red, yellow, and blue marbles. These marbles are identical in shapes. Red, yellow, and blue marbles cost $1, $2, and $3 each, respectively. Alex bought exactly 15 marbles with $34. At most how many red marbles could he have bought?

A. 11   B. 9   C. 7   D. 5   E. 3.

12. Both a and b are real numbers. Find the square root of $-ab$ if
$a^2 + 4b^2 - a + 4b + \dfrac{5}{4} = 0$.

A. 1/2   B. $-1/4$ C. 1/4   D. -2 E. 2.

13. Suppose that a and b are positive integers such that $b^2 = a^2 + 2015$. What is the greatest possible value of $2b^2 - ab - a^2$?

(A) 3023   (B) 3035   (C) 3107   (D) 3503   (E) 3568

14. Suppose that the positive number m satisfies the equation $m - \dfrac{1}{m} = 4$. What is the value of $m^4 - \dfrac{1}{m^4}$?

(A) $144\sqrt{5}$ (B) $18\sqrt{5}$ (C) 256   (D) 321   (E) $225\sqrt{5}$

15. The greatest common factor of positive integers m and n is not 1. Find mn if $m^3 + n = 2249$.

(A) 323   (B) 676   (C) 713   (D) 737   (E) 743

16. How many positive integers less than 2015 cannot be expressed as the difference of the squares of two positive integers?

(A) 506   (B) 507   (C) 1508   (D) 1511   (E) 1008

17. How many pairs of unit squares can be chosen on a 4 by 5 array of unit squats if sharing a common side is not permitted?

(A) 100   (B) 125   (C) 149   (D) 155   (E) 160

18. In how many ways can a family of seven people be seated at a round table if the youngest kid must sit between the parents?
(A) 10   (B) 12   (C) 16   (D) 24   (E) 48

19. As shown in the figure below, each of the five regions of A, B, C, D, and E will be colored by using one color choosing from 4 different colors. If no two regions next to each other have the same color, how many ways to do coloring?

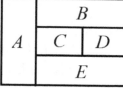

(A) 120   (B) 220   (C) 360   (D) 420   (E) 720

20. Some new train stations are added to a train line. The number of different types of new tickets between any two stations is increase by 74 (two tickets are the same if they have the same boarding station and the same destination station). What is the total number of stations for the train line after the addition?

(A) 12   (B) 14   (C) 16   (D) 18   (E) 20

21. Right triangle ABC has one leg of length 9 cm, one leg of length 12 cm and a right angle at A. A square has one side on the hypotenuse of triangle ABC and a vertex on each of the two legs of triangle ABC. What is the side length of the square?

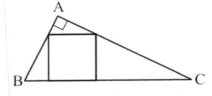

(A) $\dfrac{180}{37}$ (B) $\dfrac{90}{23}$ (C) $\dfrac{36}{5}$

(D) $\dfrac{120}{37}$ (E) $\dfrac{24}{5}$

22. In trapezoid $ABCD$, $EF \mathbin{//} BC$ and divides the trapozid into two regions of the same areas. Find the value of EF if $AD = 5\sqrt{2}$ and $BC = 12\sqrt{2}$.

A) $\dfrac{17}{2}\sqrt{2}$ (B) $13\sqrt{2}$ (C) $10\sqrt{3}$ (D) 13   (E) 16

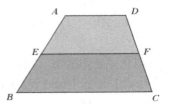

23. A list of n^2 numbers is shown in the figure. The sum of these numbers is S. What is the last two digit of S?

(A) 12   (B) 13   (C) 15   (D) 75   (E) 25

1,	2,	3,...	2015
2,	3,	4,...	2016
3,	4,	5,...	2017
....			
2015,	2016,	2017,...	4029

24. Trapezoid $ABCD$ has the area S. AB $//CD$, $AB = b$, $CD = a$ $(a < b)$. Diagonals AC and BD meet at O. If the area of $\triangle BOC$ is $\dfrac{5}{36}S$, find $\dfrac{a}{b}$.

A. 3/5   B. 2/5   C. 1/5   D. 1/2   E. 1/4.

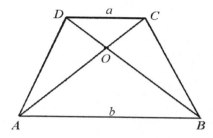

25. A, B, C are three towns forming a triangle. Alex has to walk from one to the next, ride to the next, and drive to his starting point. He can walk, ride, and drive one mile in a, b, c minutes respectively. If he starts from B he takes $a + c - b$ hours. If he starts from C, he takes $b + a - c$ hours, and if he starts from A he takes $c + b - a$ hours. Find the length of the circuit.

(A) 120   (B) 100   (C) 80   (D) 60   (E) 50

ANSWER KEYS:

1. C.
2. C.
3. D.
4. C.
5. D.
6. B.
7. E.
8. B.
9. D.
10. C.
11. D.
12. A.
13. D.
14. A.
15. B.
16. A.
17. C.
18. E.
19. D.
20. D.
21. A
22. D.
23. D.
24. C.
25. D.

SOLUTIONS:

1. C.

Kathy pays $8 \times 0.85 \times 30 - 8 \times 0.65 \times 30 = 8 \times 30(0.85 - 0.65) = 240 \times 0.2 = 24 \times 2 = 48$ dollars more dollars than Pat.

2. C.

The stone has a volume of $60 \times 30 \times 20 = 36000$ cubic centimeters.

Suppose that after the stone is placed in the tank, the water level rises by h centimeters. Then the additional volume occupied in the tank is $200 \times 60 \times h = 12000h$ cubic centimeters. Since this must be the same as the volume of the stone, we have $36000 = 12000h$ and $h = 3$ centimeters

3. D.

Let the three integers be $2x - 1$, $2x + 1$, and $2x + 3$.

Then: $2x + 3 = 5(2x - 1)$ $\Rightarrow$ $2x + 3 = 10x - 5$ $\Rightarrow$ $x = 1$

Thus the sum of three integers is be $2x - 1 + 2x + 1 + 2x + 3 = 6x + 3 = 9$.

4. C.

Let g, b, and r be the number of green, blue, and red marbles respectively.

$g + b = 12$ (1)

$r + b = 16$ (2)

$r + g = 8$ (3)

$(1) + (2 + (3): 2g + 2r + 2b = 36$ $\Rightarrow$ $g + r + b = 18$.

5. D.

Let x represent the number of children in the family and y represent the sum of the ages of all the family members. The average age of the members of the family is 17, and the average age of the members when the 35-year-old mother is not included is 14, so

$\dfrac{y}{x+2} = 17$ $\Rightarrow$ $17x - y + 34 = 0$ (1)

$\dfrac{y-35}{x+1} = 14$ $\Rightarrow$ $14x - y + 49 = 0$ (2)

(1) – (2): $3x - 15 = 0$ $\Rightarrow$ $x = 5$.

6. B.
Each vertex appears on exactly three faces, so the sum of the numbers on all the faces is

$$3(3 + 4 + 5 + 6 + 7 + 8 + 9 + 10) = 3 \times \frac{(3 + 10) \times 8}{2} = 156$$

There are six faces for the cube, so the common sum must be $156 \div 6 = 26$.
A possible numbering is shown in the figure.

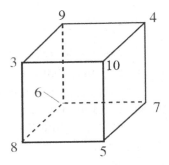

7. E.
Let C be the sum of the ages of his three children.

	x years ago	Now
Jake's age:	$X - Y$	X
His children's age:	$C - 3Y$	C

Jake's age is X years, which is also the sum of the ages of his two children: $X = C$ (1)

His age Y years ago was three times the sum of their ages then: $X - Y = 3(C - 3Y)$ (2)

Substituting (1) into (2): $X - Y = 3(X - 3Y)$ $\Rightarrow$ $X - Y = 3X - 9Y$ $\Rightarrow$
$9Y - Y = 3X - X$ $\Rightarrow$ $8Y = 2X$ $\Rightarrow$ $X/Y = 4$.

8. B.
Let the sides of the triangle have lengths $5x$, $12x$, and $13x$. The triangle is a right triangle, so its hypotenuse is a diameter of the circle. Thus $13x = 2 \times 26$, so $x = 4$. The area of the triangle is $(5 \times 4) \times (12 \times 4) / 2 = 480$.

9. D.
Method 1:
Let B be the event that the sum is greater than 14.

A_1 be the event that the first number is 6.
B_1 be the event that the second number is 9 after A_1

A_2 be the event that the first number is 7.
B_2 be the event that the second number is 8 or 9 after A_2
A_3 be the event that the first number is 8.
B_3 be the event that the second number is 7 or 9 after A_3.

A_4 be the event that the first number is 9.
B_4 be the event that the second number is 6, 7 or 8 after A_4.

Then $B = A_1B_1 + A_2B_2 + A_3B_3 + A_4B_4$

$P(B) = P(A_1B_1) + P(A_2B_2) + P(A_3B_3) + P(A_4B_4)$

$= P(A_1)P(B_1|A_1) + P(A_2)P(B_2|A_2) + P(A_3)P(B_3|A_3) + P(A_4)P(B_4|A_4)$

We know that there is 1/10 of chance to pick up the first number i ($i = 0, 9$). So $P(A_1) = 1/10$.

We know that when the first number is 5, the second number must be 9 from the set $\{0, 1, 2m\ 3, 4, 6, 7, 8, 9\}$. So $P(B_1) = 1/9$. Similarly, $P(B_2) = 2/9$, $P(B_3) = 2/9$, and $P(B_4) = 3/9$.

Therefore $P(B) = \dfrac{1}{10}(\dfrac{1}{9} + \dfrac{2}{9} + \dfrac{2}{9} + \dfrac{3}{9}) = \dfrac{1}{10} \times \dfrac{8}{9} = \dfrac{4}{45}$.

Method 2:

We have $\begin{pmatrix} 10 \\ 1 \end{pmatrix}\begin{pmatrix} 9 \\ 1 \end{pmatrix} = 90$ ways to select two distinct numbers.

When the first number is 9, we have 3 ways to select the second numbers: 8, 7, or 6.
When the first number is 8, we have 2 ways to select the second numbers: 9, or 7.
When the first number is 7, we have 2 ways to select the second numbers: 9, or 8.
When the first number is 6, we have 1 way to select the second numbers: 9.
When the first number is less than 6, we have no ways to select the second numbers.

So the numerator is $3 + 2 + 2 + 1 = 8$.

The answer is $P = \dfrac{8}{90} = \dfrac{4}{45}$.

10. C.
Connect AC and BF. It is easy to see that $\angle EBF = \angle ECA = 45°$. Thus we know that $AC \parallel BF$ and $S_{\triangle AOF} = S_{\triangle BOC}$

So the area of the shaded region is the same as the area of the quarter circle.

The answer is then $\dfrac{\pi \times 10^2}{4} = 25\pi$.

11. D.
Let x, y, and z be the number of red, yellow, and blue marbles he could buy, respectively.
$x + y + z = 15$ (1)
$x + 2y + 3z = 34$ (2)
$(1) \times 3 - (2)$: $2x - y = 11$ $\Rightarrow$ $y = 11 - 2x$

Since y is a nonnegative integer, the greatest value of x can be 5.

12. A.

$$a^2 + 4b^2 - a + 4b + \frac{5}{4} = 0 \quad \Rightarrow \quad (a^2 - a) + (4b^2 + 4b) + \frac{5}{4} = 0 \quad \Rightarrow$$

$$[a^2 - 2 \times \frac{1}{2}a + (\frac{1}{2})^2 - (\frac{1}{2})^2] + (4b^2 + 2 \times 2b \times 1 + 1^2 - 1^2) + \frac{5}{4} = 0$$

$$\Rightarrow \quad (a - \frac{1}{2})^2 + (2b - 1^2) - \frac{1}{4} + \frac{5}{4} - 1 = 0 \Rightarrow (a - \frac{1}{2})^2 + (2b - 1^2) = 0.$$

Since $(a - \frac{1}{2})^2 \geq 0$, and $(2b - 1^2) \geq 0$, we have $a = \frac{1}{2}$ and $b = -\frac{1}{2}$.

$-ab = -\frac{1}{2} \times (-\frac{1}{2}) = \frac{1}{4}$. Therefore $\sqrt{-ab} = \sqrt{-(\frac{1}{2})(-\frac{1}{2})} = \sqrt{\frac{1}{4}} = \frac{1}{2}$.

13. D.

$$b^2 = a^2 + 2015 \quad \Rightarrow \quad b^2 - a^2 = 2015 \quad \Rightarrow$$
$$(b - a)(b + a) = 5 \times 13 \times 31 = 1 \times 2015 = 5 \times 403 = 13 \times 155 = 31 \times 65$$

We know that $b + a \geq b - a$.

$$\left. \begin{array}{l} b + a = 2015 \\ b - a = 1 \end{array} \right\} \quad \Longrightarrow \quad b = 1008, a = 1007$$

$$\left. \begin{array}{l} b + a = 403 \\ b - a = 5 \end{array} \right\} \quad \Longrightarrow \quad b = 204, a = 199$$

$$\left. \begin{array}{l} b + a = 155 \\ b - a = 13 \end{array} \right\} \quad \Longrightarrow \quad b = 84, a = 71$$

$$\left. \begin{array}{l} b + a = 65 \\ b - a = 31 \end{array} \right\} \quad \Longrightarrow \quad b = 48, a = 17$$

$$2b^2 - ab - a^2 = (2b + a)(b - a)$$
$$= (2 \times 1008 + 1007)(1008 - 1007) = 3023$$

$$= (2 \times 204 + 199)(204 - 199) = 3035$$
$$= (2 \times 84 + 71)(84 - 71) = 3107$$
$$= (2 \times 48 + 17)(48 - 17) = 3503$$

Method 2:

We know that $b + a \geq b - a$. We also want the greatest value of $2b^2 - ab - a^2 = (2b + a)(b - a)$. So the difference of b and a should be as large as possible.

$$\left. \begin{array}{l} b + a = 65 \\ b - a = 31 \end{array} \right\} \quad \Longrightarrow \quad b = 48, \, a = 17$$

$2b^2 - ab - a^2 = (2b + a)(b - a) = (2 \times 48 + 17)(48 - 17) = 3503$.

14. A.

Squaring both sides of $m - \dfrac{1}{m} = 4$: $(m - \dfrac{1}{m})^2 = 16 \Rightarrow \left(m^2 + \dfrac{1}{m^2}\right) = 18$.

We also have $\left(m^2 + \dfrac{1}{m^2}\right) = 18 \Rightarrow m^2 + \dfrac{1}{m^2} + 2 = 18 + 2 \quad \Rightarrow$

$m^2 + \dfrac{1}{m^2} + 2m \times \dfrac{1}{m} = 20 \Rightarrow \quad (m + \dfrac{1}{m})^2 = 20 \quad \Rightarrow \quad (m + \dfrac{1}{m}) = 2\sqrt{5}$

$m^4 - \dfrac{1}{m^4} = \left(m^2 - \dfrac{1}{m^2}\right)\left(m^2 + \dfrac{1}{m^2}\right) = 18\left(m^2 - \dfrac{1}{m^2}\right) = 18(m - \dfrac{1}{m})(m + \dfrac{1}{m})$

$= 18 \times 4 \times \sqrt{5} = 144\sqrt{5}$.

15. B.

Let k be the greatest common factor of m and n.

$m = ka$

$n = kb \ (k > 1)$

$m^3 + n = 2249 \Rightarrow \quad (ka)^3 + kb = 2249 \quad \Rightarrow \quad k(k^2a^3 + b) = 13 \times 173$

We know that $k > 1$, $k^2a^3 + b > k^2a^3 > k^2 > k$, and 13 and 173 are relatively prime. We have $k = 13$ and $k^2a^3 + b = 173$.

Thus $k^2a^3 + b = 173 \quad \Rightarrow \quad 13^2a^3 + b = 173 \quad \Rightarrow \quad 169a^3 + b = 173$.

Since both a and b are positive integers, we have $a = 1$ and $b = 4$.
So $m = 13$ and $n = 52$. $mn = 676$.

16. A.
Let two square numbers be m^2 and n^2.
Let x be the number such that $m^2 - n^2 = (m - n)(m + n) = x$, $(1 \leq x \leq 2014)$, m and n are positive integers.

We know that m and n are both even or are both odd. If m and n are both even, x is divisible by 4; If m and n are both odd, x is odd.

Thus any number that can be expressed as the difference of two square numbers must be either a multiple of 4 or an odd positive integer.

There are $2014/2 = 1007$ odd numbers and $\left\lfloor \dfrac{2014}{4} \right\rfloor = 503$ multiples of 4.

Note that $4t = (t + 1)^2 - (t - 1)^2$. So the case $t = 1$ (the number 4) should be removed.

Also $2t + 1 = (t + 1)^2 - t^2$. So the case $t = 0$ (the number 1) should be removed.
The answer is $2014 - (1007 + 503 - 1 - 1) = 2014 - 1508 = 506$.

17. C.
We have two cases that a pair of squares share the same side: one by two or two by one.

We count $4 \times 4 = 26$ one by two pairs

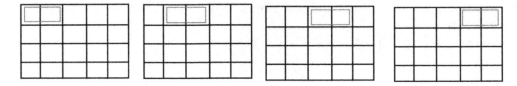

and $3 \times 5 = 15$ two by one pairs .

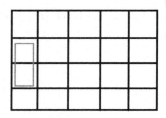
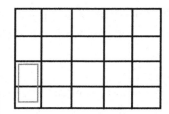

The total number of pairs is $\binom{20}{2} = 190$.

The answer is $190 - 26 - 15 = 149$.

18. E.

We link two parents and the youngest kid together to form a unit. There are $(5 - 1)!$ ways to seat them at the table. The result must be multiplied by 2 since we can switch the positions of the two parents. The solution is $(5 - 1)! \times 2 = 48$.

19. D.

First we assume that we color the regions by the order of A、B、C、D、E. Since A and D are not neighboring regions, they can have the same color or different color.

(1) If A and D have the same color, A will have 5 ways to color; B has 4 ways to color, C cannot have the same color with A or B, so C can have three ways to color, E can not have the same color as A and C, so E also has three ways to color. From the Fundamental Counting Principle, the ways=5×4×3×3=180.

(2) If A and D have different colors, A still has 5 ways to color, B still has 4 ways to color, C still has 3 ways to color, D has different color with A, B, and C, so D only has 2 ways to color. E cannot have the same color with A, C, and D, so E has 2 ways to color., From the Fundamental Counting Principle, the ways = 5 × 4 × 3 × 2 × 2 = 240.
Total ways to color: 5 × 4 × 3 × 3 + 5 × 4 × 3 × 2 × 2 = 420.

20. D.

Let x be the number of old stations, and y be the number of new stations.

$P(x+y,2) - P(x,2) = 74$.

P is the symbol of permutation.

$(x+y)(x+y) - 1) - x(x-1) = 745$

$y(2x+y-1) = 74$

We know that $2x+y-1-y = 2x+1 > 0$. So $y < 2x+y-1$.

$y(2x+y-1) = 2 \times 37 \Rightarrow \quad y = 2 \text{ and } 2x+y-1 = 37 \quad \Rightarrow \quad 2x = 36$

$\Rightarrow \quad x = 18$

21. A

Method 1:

In $\triangle ABC$, $AB = 9$, $AC = 12$, and $BC = 15$.

Since $ED // FG$, $\triangle AED \sim \triangle ABC$

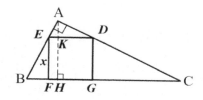

$\dfrac{AE}{ED} = \dfrac{AB}{BC} \quad \Rightarrow \quad \dfrac{AE}{x} = \dfrac{9}{15} = \dfrac{3}{5} \quad \Rightarrow \quad AE = \dfrac{3}{5}x$

$\dfrac{AD}{ED} = \dfrac{AC}{BC} \quad \Rightarrow \quad \dfrac{AD}{x} = \dfrac{12}{15} = \dfrac{4}{5} \quad \Rightarrow \quad AD = \dfrac{4}{5}x$

Draw $AH \perp BC$. AH meets ED at K.

Since $S_{\triangle ABC} = \dfrac{AB \times AC}{2} = \dfrac{BC \times AH}{2}$, $AH = \dfrac{AB \times AC}{BC} = \dfrac{9 \times 12}{15} = \dfrac{36}{5}$

Since $S_{\triangle AED} = \dfrac{AE \times AD}{2} = \dfrac{ED \times AK}{2}$, we have $\dfrac{\dfrac{3}{5}x \times \dfrac{4}{5}x}{2} = \dfrac{x \times (\dfrac{36}{5} - x)}{2} \quad \Rightarrow$

$\dfrac{3}{5} \times \dfrac{4}{5}x = \dfrac{36}{5} - x$

Solve for x: $x = \dfrac{180}{37}$.

Method 2:

In $\triangle ABC$, $AB = 9$, $AC = 12$, $BC = 15$.

Since $ED // BC$, $\triangle AED \sim \triangle ABC$

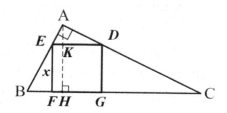

$\dfrac{AE}{ED} = \dfrac{AB}{BC} \quad \Rightarrow \quad \dfrac{AE}{x} = \dfrac{9}{15} = \dfrac{3}{5} \quad \Rightarrow$

$$AE = \frac{3}{5}x$$

Draw $AH \perp BC$. AH meets ED at K.

Since $S_{\triangle ABC} = \dfrac{AB \times AC}{2} = \dfrac{BC \times AH}{2}$, $AH = \dfrac{AB \times AC}{BC} = \dfrac{9 \times 12}{15} = \dfrac{36}{5}$

Since $EK//BH$, $\triangle AEK \sim \triangle ABH$, $\dfrac{AE}{AB} = \dfrac{AK}{AH}$.

$$\frac{\frac{3}{5}x}{9} = \frac{\frac{36}{5}-x}{\frac{36}{5}} \quad \Rightarrow \quad \frac{x}{15} \times \frac{36}{5} = \frac{36}{5} - x$$

Solve for x: $x = \dfrac{180}{37}$.

Method 3:

In $\triangle ABC$, $AB = 9$, $AC = 12$, and $BC = 15$.

Draw $AH \perp BC$. AH meets ED at K and BC at H.

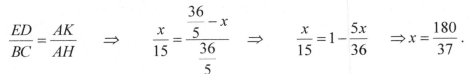

Since $S_{\triangle ABC} = \dfrac{AB \times AC}{2} = \dfrac{BC \times AH}{2}$,

$$AH = \frac{AB \times AC}{BC} = \frac{9 \times 12}{15} = \frac{36}{5}$$

Since $ED//BC$, $\triangle AED \sim \triangle ABC$

$$\frac{ED}{BC} = \frac{AK}{AH} \quad \Rightarrow \quad \frac{x}{15} = \frac{\frac{36}{5}-x}{\frac{36}{5}} \quad \Rightarrow \quad \frac{x}{15} = 1 - \frac{5x}{36} \quad \Rightarrow x = \frac{180}{37}.$$

Method 4:

Theorem: Square $DEFG$ inscribes in $\triangle ABC$, $\angle A = 90°$. If $AB = a$, $AC = b$, then
$BF : FG : GC = a^2 : ab : b^2$

In our case, $AB = 9$, $AC = 12$, and $BC = 15$.

$BF : FG : GC = AB^2 : AB \times AC : AC^2 = 9^2 : 9 \times 12 : 15^2$

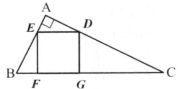

$$FG = \frac{9 \times 12}{9^2 + 9 \times 12 + 12^2} \times BC = \frac{108}{414} \times 15 = \frac{180}{37}.$$

22. D.

Extend BA and CD to meet at P. Since $AD//EF$,
$\triangle PAD \sim \triangle PEF$.

We have $\dfrac{S_{\triangle PAD}}{AD^2} = \dfrac{S_{\triangle PEF}}{EF^2}$.

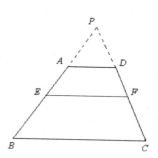

Similarly, we have $\dfrac{S_{\triangle PEF}}{EF^2} = \dfrac{S_{\triangle PBC}}{BC^2} = \dfrac{S_{\triangle PAD}}{AD^2} = k$.

So $S_{\triangle PAD} = k \times AD^2 \quad S_{\triangle PEF} = k \times EF^2 \quad S_{\triangle ABC} = k \times BC^2$

Since $S_{ADFE} = S_{EFCB}$, $S_{\triangle PEF} - S_{\triangle PAD} = S_{\triangle PBC} - S_{\triangle PEF}$.

Or $k \times EF^2 - k \times AD^2 = k \times BC^2 - k \times EF^2$.

Dividing each term by k yields $AD^2 + BC^2 = 2EF^2$ or

$$EF^2 = \frac{(5\sqrt{2})^2 + (12\sqrt{2})^2}{2} = 13^2$$

$EF = 13$.

23. D.

Method 1:

The sum of all numbers in the first row is $\dfrac{2015(2015+1)}{2}$.

In the second row, every number is 1 more than the number above it. So the sum of the numbers in the second row is 2015 more than the sum of the numbers in the first row. The pattern continues for every row.

Thus the sum of the number in each row form an arithmetic sequence with the

first term $\dfrac{2015(2015+1)}{2}$ and common difference 2015: $\dfrac{2015(2015+1)}{2}$,

$\dfrac{2015(2015+1)}{2} + 2015$, $\dfrac{2015(2015+1)}{2} + 2015 \times 2$,...., $\dfrac{2015(2015+1)}{2} + 2015$

$\times 2014$.

So the final sum is

$$S = \frac{n}{2}[2a_1 + (n-1)d)] = 2015 \times \frac{2015(2015+1)}{2} + \frac{2015(2015-1)}{2} \times 2015 = 2015^3.$$

The last two digits of 2015^3 are the same as the last digit of 15^3, which are 75.

24. C.

Let the area of $\triangle DOC$ be S_1 and the area of $\triangle AOB$ be S_2.

We have

$$\begin{cases} S_1 + S_2 = S - (\frac{5}{36}S) \times 2 = \frac{26}{36}S \\ S_1 S_2 = (\frac{5}{36}S)^2 \end{cases}$$

Solving for S_1 and S_2, we get $\begin{cases} S_1 = \frac{25}{36}S \\ S_2 = \frac{1}{36}S \end{cases}$ or $\begin{cases} S_1 = \frac{1}{36}S \\ S_2 = \frac{25}{36}S \end{cases}$.

Since $a < b$, then $S_1 < S_2$. Therefore $\dfrac{a}{b} = \sqrt{\dfrac{S_1}{S_2}} = \sqrt{\dfrac{\frac{1}{36}S}{\frac{25}{36}S}} = \sqrt{\dfrac{1}{25}} = \dfrac{1}{5}$.

25. D.

If he can walk a mile in a minute, his speed is $\dfrac{60}{a}$ mph.

Similarly his riding speed is $\dfrac{60}{b}$, and driving speed is $\dfrac{60}{c}$.

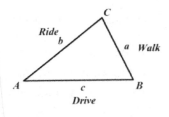

$$\frac{BC}{\frac{60}{a}} + \frac{CA}{\frac{60}{b}} + \frac{AB}{\frac{60}{c}} = a + c - b \qquad (1)$$

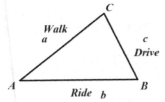

144

$$\dfrac{\dfrac{CA}{60}}{a} + \dfrac{\dfrac{AB}{60}}{b} + \dfrac{\dfrac{BC}{60}}{c} = b + a - c \qquad\qquad (2)$$

$$\dfrac{\dfrac{AB}{60}}{a} + \dfrac{\dfrac{BC}{60}}{b} + \dfrac{\dfrac{CA}{60}}{c} = c + b - a \qquad\qquad (3)$$

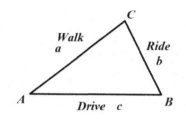

$(1) + (2) + (3)$:

$$(A + B + C)(\dfrac{a}{60} + \dfrac{b}{60} + \dfrac{c}{60}) = a + b + c$$

$\Rightarrow \qquad A + B + C = 60$ miles.

American Mathematics Competitions

Practice 9
AMC 10

(American Mathematics Contest 10)

INSTRUCTIONS

1. This is a twenty-five question multiple choice test. Each question is followed by answers marked A, B, C, D and E. Only one of these is correct.

2. You will have 75 minutes to complete the test.

3. No aids are permitted other than scratch paper, graph paper, rulers, and erasers. No problems on the test will require the use of a calculator.

4. Figures are not necessarily drawn to scale.

5. SCORING: You will receive 6 points for each correct answer, 1.5 points for each problem left unanswered, and 0 points for each incorrect answer.

1. A bakery owner turns on his doughnut machine at 7:30 am. At 9:10 am the machine has completed two third of the day's job. At what time will the doughnut machine complete four fifth of the job?

(A) 9:30 pm   (B) 9: 20 am   (C) 9: 25 am   (D) 9:30 am   (E) 9: 15 am

2. Taylor had 123 marbles and Eric had 12 marbles. Taylor then gave some of his marbles to Eric so that Taylor had four times as many marbles as Eric had. How many marbles did Taylor give to Eric?

(A) 3   (B) 13   (C) 15   (D) 18   (E) 28

3. A drawer contains red, green, blue and white socks with at least 3 of each color.
What is the minimum number of socks that must be pulled from the drawer to guarantee two matching pairs?

(A) 4   (B) 5   (C) 7   (D) 8   (E) 9

4. The area of a circle whose circumference is 36π is $k\pi$. What is the value of k ?

(A) 136   (B) 272   (C) 294   (D) 316   (E) 324

5. A month with 31 days has the same number of Tuesdays and Thursdays. How many of the seven days of the week could be the first day of this month?

(A) 1   (B) 2   (C) 3   (D) 4   (E) 5

6. An ant moves along the sides of an equilateral triangle. The speeds the ant moves in three sides are 20 cm per minutes, 40 cm per minutes, and 50 cm per minutes, respectively. What is the ant's average speed in cm per minute if the ant moves one complete loop?

(A) $31\dfrac{11}{19}$ (B) $31\dfrac{11}{18}$ (C) $21\dfrac{11}{19}$ (D) $31\dfrac{12}{19}$ (E) $11\dfrac{11}{19}$

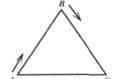

7. On the number line above, the tick marks are equally spaced. What is the value of $y - x$?

(A) 4/5   (B) 3/4   (C) 2/5   (D) 1/4   (E) 1/5

8. A circle is centered at O, AB is a diameter and C is a point on the circle with $\angle COB = 44°$. What is the degree measure of $\angle OCA$?

(A) 20°   (B) 22°   (C) 25°   (D) 56°   (E) 88°

9. A ticket to a school play costs x dollars, where x is a whole number. A group of girls buys tickets costing a total of $444, and a group of boys buys tickets costing a total of $792. How many values for x are possible?

(A) 3   (B) 5   (C) 8   (D) 10   (E) 6

10. Select any positive integer, a. If a is even, divide a by 2 to get the next number; if a is odd, multiply a by 3 then add 1 to get the next number. Repeating the process, what is the 2015th term in the sequence produced if the starting number is $a = 52$?

(A) 1   (B) 2   (C) 3   (D) 4   (E) 5

11. While Steven and Tom are fishing 2 mile from shore, their boat springs a leak, and water comes in at a constant rate of 12 gallons per minute. The boat will sink if it takes in more than 72 gallons of water. Steven starts rowing toward the shore at a constant rate of 5 miles per hour while Tom bails water out of the boat. What is the slowest rate, in gallons per minute, at which Tom can bail if they are to reach the shore without sinking?

(A) 3   (B) 6   (C) 9   (D) 12   (E) 13

12. In a collection of red, blue, and green marbles, there are 12.5% more red marbles than blue marbles, and there are $11\frac{1}{9}$% more green marbles than red marbles. Suppose that there are r red marbles. What is the total number of marbles in the collection?

(A) $3r$ (B) $2r$ (C) $4r$ (D) $5r$ (E) $6r$

13. The greatest common factor and the least common multiple of the length and width of a rectangle are 7 and 140, respectively. Find the smallest possible value of the perimeter if the length and width are all positive integers.

(A) 72   (B) 86   (C) 98   (D) 126   (E) 132

14. Alex and Bob are assigned to do a particular job. It is known that Bob can do 50% more work each day than Alex. Let t be the total time, in days, required for them to complete the job working together. If Alex starts the job alone and completes 3/5 of the job and left, and Bob continues to finish the job, the total time will be $t + 7$ days. Which of the following numbers could be t?

(A) 3   (B) 10   (C) 9   (D) 6   (E) 11

15. A regular pentagon has side length 6. What is the area of the region containing all points that are outside the pentagon and not more than 3 units from a point of the pentagon?

(A) $90 + 9\pi$ (B) $90 + \pi$ (C) $18 + 9\pi$ (D) $90 + 2\pi$ (E) 117

16. In the right triangle ABC shown, E and D are the trisection points of the hypotenuse AB. If $CD = 7$ and $CE = 6$, what is the area of triangle ABC?

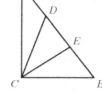

(A) $6\sqrt{38}$ (B) $\frac{4}{3}\sqrt{38}$ (C) $7\sqrt{38}$ (D) $8\sqrt{38}$ (E) $\frac{6}{5}\sqrt{38}$

17. Compute $2013 \times 20152015 - 2015 \times 20132012$.

(A) 2012   (B) 2013   (C) 2015   (D) 2016   (E) 1

18. Four fair, standard six-faced dice of different colors are rolled. In how many ways can the dice be rolled such that the sum of the numbers rolled is 20?

(A) 20   (B) 25   (C) 30   (D) 35   (E) 40

19. The faces of a cubical die are marked with the numbers 1, 2, 2, 3, 3, and 4. The faces of a second cubical die are marked with the numbers 1, 3, 4, 5, 6, and 8. Both dice are thrown. What is the probability that the sum of the two top numbers will be 6, 8, or 10 ?

(A) 7/18   (B) 13/36   (C) 11/18   (D) 11/36   (E) 3/5

20. Four red beads, three white beads, and one blue bead are placed in a line in random order. What is the probability that no two neighboring beads are the same color?

(A) 1/10   (B) 1/14   (C) 1/16   (D) 1/18   (E) 1/20

21. The triangular grid of equilateral triangles shown below contains a shaded equilateral triangle. What is the probability that a randomly selected equilateral triangular sub-region contains the shaded area?

(A) 8/27   (B) 9/29   (C) 2/9   (D) 1/3   (E) 7/27

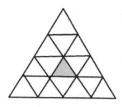

22. How many 3-digit numbers are there such that the sum of the digits is 17?

(A) 31   (B) 45   (C) 57   (D) 61   (E) 63

23. Circle A of radius 4 is inscribed in a semicircle. Two congruent circles B and C are tangent to circle A and the semicircle, as shown. The area inside the semicircle but outside the three circles is shaded. What fraction of the semicircle's area is shaded?

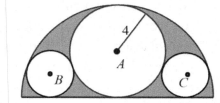

(A) 1/2   (B) 1/3   (C) 1/4   (D) 1/5   (E) 2/3

24. Given trapezoid $ABCD$ with $AB//DC$. CE is the angle bisector of $\angle BCD$. CE $\perp AD$. $DE = 2AE$. CE cuts the trapezoid $ABCD$ into two parts of areas S_1 and S_2. If $S_1 = 28$, find S_2.

A. 38   B. 25   C. 28   D. 32   E. 36.

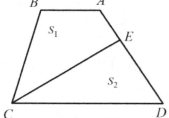

25. How many positive integers among 1 and 4030 inclusive that are multiples of 2, 5, or 13 but not 31?

(A) 2590   (B) 2015   (C) 806   (D) 130   (E) 2460

ANSWER KEYS

1. D.
2. C.
3. C.
4. E.
5. C.
6. A.
7. C.
8. B
9. E.
10. B.
11. C.
12. A.
13. D.
14. D.
15. A.
16. A.
17. C.
18. D.
19. B.
20. E.
21. D.
22. D.
23. C.
24. D.
25. E.

SOLUTIONS:

1. D.

The machine worked for 1 hour and 40 minutes, or 100 minutes, to complete two third of the job.

Let x be the time needed to complete the job.

$$\frac{100}{\frac{2}{3}} = \frac{x}{\frac{4}{5}} \qquad \Rightarrow \qquad x = \frac{4}{5} \times 150 = 120.$$

So the time is $7:30 + 2:00 = 9:30$ am to complete four fifth of the job.

2. C.

Let x be the number of marbles that Taylor gave to Eric. Then $123 - x = 4(12 + x)$. Solving this equation yields $x = 15$.

3. C.

If a set of 4 socks does not contain a pair, there must be one of each color. The fifth sock must match one of the others and guarantee one matching pair. Let us say we got a pair of red socks now. If we are lucky, the sixth draw will match one sock of the other three colors and we are done. If we are unlucky, the sixth draw will be the red sock and we still do not have two matching pairs yet. But the seventh draw will guarantee two matching pairs.

4. E.

Because the circumference is $2\pi r = 36\pi$, the radius r is 18.
Therefore the area is $\pi r^2 = 324\pi$, and $k = 324$.

5. C.

A month with 31 days has 3 successive days of the week appearing five times and 4 successive days of the week appearing four times. If Tuesday and Thursday appear five times then Tuesday must be the first day of the month. If Tuesday and Thursday appear only four times then either Friday or Saturday must be the first day of the month. Hence there are 3 days of the week that could be the first day of the month.

6. A.

Method 1:

We assume that the length of each side is 200 cm.

The time needed to move one loop is $t = \dfrac{200}{20} + \dfrac{200}{40} + \dfrac{200}{50} = 19$ minutes.

Therefore the average speed is $r = \dfrac{600}{19} = 31\dfrac{11}{19}$.

Method 2:

The harmonic mean of the three speeds is $r = \dfrac{3}{\dfrac{1}{20} + \dfrac{1}{40} + \dfrac{1}{50}} = 31\dfrac{11}{19}$ cm per minute.

7. C.

The whole is 5/5. x indicates 1/5 and y indicates 3/5. Therefore $y - x = \dfrac{3}{5} - \dfrac{1}{5} = \dfrac{2}{5}$.

8. B.

Note that $\angle CAB$ is half of $\angle COB$ so $\angle CAB = 44°/2 = 22°$. Since $AO = CO$ (radius), $\triangle AOC$ is isosceles, $\angle OCA = \angle OAC = \angle CAB = 22°$.

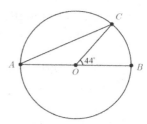

9. E.

The cost of an individual ticket must divide 444 and 792. The common factors of 444 and 792 are 1, 2, 3, 4, 6, and 12. Each of these may be the cost of one ticket, so there are 6 possible values for x.

10. B.

52, 26, 13, 40, 20, 10, 5, 16, 8, 4, 2, 1, 4, 2, 1, ...

We see that after 9 terms in the sequence, the pattern is 4, 2, 1; 4, 2, 1;...
2015 − 9 = 2006.
2006 ÷ 3 = 668 r 2. So the 2015th term in the sequence is 2.

11. C.

At the rate of 5 miles per hour, Steven can row 2 miles in 24 minutes. During that time 24 × 12 = 288 gallons of water will enter the boat. Tom must bail 288 − 72 = 216 gallons of water during that time. So he must bail at the rate of at least 216/24 = 9 gallons per minute.

12. A.

Let b and g represent the number of blue and green marbles, respectively. Then r = (1 + 12.5%)b and $g = (1 + 11\frac{1}{9}\%)r$. Thus the total number of red, blue, and green marbles is

$$r + b + g = r + \frac{r}{1 + 12.5\%} + (1 + 11\frac{1}{9}\%)r = r + \frac{r}{1 + \frac{1}{8}} + \frac{10}{9}r = r(1 + \frac{8}{9} + \frac{10}{9}) = 3r$$

13. D.

Let a be the length and b be the width of the rectangle, and P be the area.
7 × 140 = ab

ab = 7 × 140 = 980 = 2^2 × 5 × 7^2 = 1 × 980 = 2 × 490 = 4 × 245= 5 × 196 = 7 × 140 = 10 × 98 = 14 × 70 = 28 × 35.

Since we want the smallest possible value of the perimeter, the values of a and b must be as close as possible.

The smallest perimeter is P = 2(28 + 35) = 2 × 63 = 126.

14. D.

Let x be the number of days for Bob to finish the job alone, $\frac{3}{2}x$ be the number of days for Alex to finish the job alone.

Since t is the total time, in days, required for them to complete the job working together, we have $(\frac{1}{x} + \frac{1}{\frac{3}{2}x})t = 1$ $\Rightarrow$ $(\frac{1}{x} + \frac{2}{3x})t = 1$ $\Rightarrow$ $5t = 3x$ (1)

Let t_1 be the time needed for Alex to do 3/5 of the job, we have $\frac{1}{\frac{3}{2}x}t_1 = \frac{3}{5}$ (2)

Let t_2 be the time needed for Bob to do 2/5 of the job. We have $\frac{1}{x}t_2 = \frac{2}{5}$ (3)

We also know that $t_1 + t_2 = t + 7$ (4)

From (2), we have $t_1 = \frac{3}{5} \times \frac{3}{2}x = \frac{9}{10}x$ (5)

From (3), we have $t_2 = \frac{2}{5}x$ (6)

(5) + (6): $t_1 + t_2 = \frac{9}{10}x + \frac{2}{5}x = \frac{13}{10}x$ (7)

Substituting (7) into (4): $\frac{13}{10}x = t + 7$ $\Rightarrow$ $t = \frac{13}{10}x - 7$ (8)

Substituting (8) into (1): $5(\frac{13}{10}x - 7) = 3x$ $\Rightarrow$ $x = 10$. Then $t = 13 - 7 = 6$.

15. A.

The region consists of five rectangles with length 6 and width 3 together with five 72° sectors of circles with radius 3.

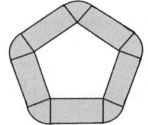

The combined area of the five 72° sectors is the same as the area of a circle with radius 3, so the area of the region is $5(3 \times 6) + \pi \times 3^2 = 90 + 9\pi$.

16. A.

Draw $DG \parallel BC$, $EF \parallel AC$ as shown.

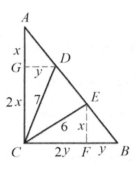

Since $AD = EB$, $\angle ADG = \angle EBF$, $\angle GAD = \angle FEB$, $\triangle ADG$ is congruent to $\triangle EBF$.

Let $AG = EF = x$ and $GD = BF = y$.
$CG = 2x$ and $CF = 2y$.

Applying Pythagorean Theorem to right triangle CDG :
$$(2x)^2 + y^2 = 7^2 \qquad (1)$$

Applying Pythagorean Theorem to right triangle CFE: $(2y)^2 + x^2 = 6^2 \qquad (2)$

(1) + (2): $5x^2 + 5y^2 = 7^2 + 6^2 = 85 \Rightarrow x^2 + y^2 = 17$.

$\Rightarrow y^2 = 17 - x^2 \qquad\qquad\qquad (3)$

Substituting (3) into (1): $3x^2 = 32 \quad \Rightarrow \quad x^2 = \dfrac{32}{3}$. Then

$y^2 = 17 - x^2 = 17 - \dfrac{32}{3} = \dfrac{19}{3}$.

Thus $x^2 y^2 = \dfrac{32}{3} \times \dfrac{19}{3} \quad \Rightarrow \quad xy = \dfrac{4}{3}\sqrt{38}$.

The area of triangle ABC is $\dfrac{9xy}{2} = \dfrac{9}{2} \times \dfrac{4}{3}\sqrt{38} = 6\sqrt{38}$

17. C.
Method 1:
$2013 \times 20152015 - 2015 \times 20132012$
$= \ 2015(2013 \times 10001 - 20132012)$
$= \ 2015(20132013 - 20132012) = 2015$

Method 2:
Let 2013 be n.
The original expression becomes:
$n[(n+2) \times 10^4 + (n+2)] - (n+2)[n \times 10^4 + (n-1)]$
$= \ n(n+2) \times 10^4 + n(n+2) - n(n+2) \times 10^4 - (n+2)(n-1)]$
$= \ n(n+2) - (n+2)(n-1)] \ = \ n(n+2) - n(n+2) + (n+2) = n+2$
$= \ 2013 + 2 = 2015.$

18. D.
Method 1:
 We list:

6	6	6	2	$\dfrac{4!}{3!} = 4$
6	6	5	3	$\dfrac{4!}{2!} = 12$
6	6	4	4	$\dfrac{4!}{2!2!} = 6$
6	5	5	4	$\dfrac{4!}{2!} = 12$
5	5	5	5	$\dfrac{4!}{4!} = 1$

$4 + 12 + 6 + 12 + 1 = 35.$

Method 2:
$$x_1 + x_2 + x_3 + x_4 = 20 \qquad (1 \le x_i \le 6)$$

$$N = \binom{20-1}{4-1} - \binom{4}{1}\binom{20-6-1}{4-1} + \binom{4}{2}\binom{20-2\times6-1}{4-1} = 35.$$

Method 3: This problem is the same as "How many nonnegative solutions are there to the equation $x_1 + x_2 + x_3 + x_4 = 4$?"

$$N = \binom{4+4-1}{4-1} = \binom{7}{3} = 35.$$

19. B.

Of the 36 possible outcomes, the five pairs (1, 5), (2, 4), (2, 4), (3, 3), and (3, 3) yield a sum of 6. The five pairs (2, 6), (2, 6), (3, 5), (3, 5), and (4, 4) yield a sum of 8. The three pairs (2, 8), (2, 8), and (4, 6) yield a sum of 10. Thus the probability of getting a sum of 6, 8, or 10 is (5 + 5 + 3)/36 = 13/36.

20. E.

There are 8!/(4!3!1!) = 280 distinguishable orders of the beads on the line. To meet the required condition, we have the following configurations:
Case 1:

We have $\dfrac{4!}{3!} \times 2 = 8$ configurations

Case 1 *a*   Case 1 *b*

Case 2:

We have $2 \times 3 = 6$ configurations

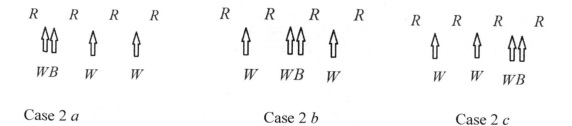

Case 2 *a*   Case 2 *b*   Case 2 *c*

Hence there are 8 + 6 = 14 orders that meet the required condition.
The probability is 14/280 = 1/20.

21. D.

Method 1:

The total number of equilateral triangles is

$$N = \frac{n(n+2)(2n+1)}{8} = 27$$

The number of triangular sub-regions that contain the shaded area is

$$\binom{2}{1} \times \binom{2}{1} \times \binom{2}{1} + 1 = 9$$

The probability equals 9/27 = 1/3.

Note:

$$N = \frac{n(n+2)(2n+1)}{8} \text{ for even } n \qquad N = \frac{n(n+2)(2n+1)-1}{8} \text{ for odd } n$$

Method 2:

We count the total number of equilateral triangles: $16 + 7 + 3 + 1 = 27$.
The number of triangular sub-regions that contain the shaded area is 89.
The total number of equilateral triangles is 27.

The probability equals 9/27 = 1/3.

22. D.

Method 1:

To find the number of solutions to $x_1 + x_2 + x_3 = 17$ with restrictions $1 \leq x_1 \leq 9$, $0 \leq x_2 \leq 9$, and $0 \leq x_3 \leq 9$, we first calculate the number of positive integer solutions:

$$N_1 = \binom{17-1}{2} - \binom{3}{1}\binom{17-9-1}{2} = \binom{16}{2} - 3\binom{7}{2} = 120 - 3 \times 21 = 57.$$

We then calculate N_2, the number of positive integers containing zero in the ten's and units digits by listing:

9   8   0   (4 rearrangements)

So $N_2 = 4$

$N = N_1 + N_2 = 57 + 4 = 61$.

Method 2:

The number of solutions to the equation: $x_1 + x_2 + x_3 = 17$ (with the restrictions $1 \le x_1 \le 9$, and $0 \le x_i \le 9$, $i = 2, 3$) is $\quad N = N_1 - N_2$.

N_1, the number of non-negative integer solutions of the above equation, equals

$$N_1 = \binom{17 + 3 - 1}{3 - 1} - \binom{3}{1}\binom{17 + 3 - 1 \times 10 - 1}{3 - 1} = 171 - 108 = 63$$

N_2, the number of non-negative integer solutions to the equation: $y_1 + y_2 = 17$ (with the restrictions $0 \le y_i \le 9$, $i = 1, 2$), equals

$$N_2 = \binom{17 + 2 - 1}{2 - 1} - \binom{2}{1}\binom{17 + 2 - 1 \times 10 - 1}{2 - 1} = 18 - 16 = 2$$

The desired solution is then $N_1 - N_2 = 63 - 2 = 61$.

23. C.

The semicircle has radius 8 and total area $\dfrac{1}{2}\pi \times (8)^2 = 32\pi$.

We connect AC. Draw $AD \perp DF$, and $CF \perp DF$. Draw $CF \parallel DF$ to meet AD at E. Connect DC and extend it to meet the semicircle at G. G is the tangent point and DCG are collinear.

Let the radius of two congruent circles be r. By Pythagorean Theorem,

$$EC^2 = AC^2 - AE^2 = DC^2 - DE^2 \quad \Rightarrow$$
$$(4 + r)^2 - (4 - r)^2 = (8 - r)^2 - r^2 \quad \Rightarrow$$
$$(4 + r + 4 - r)(4 + r - 4 + r) = (8 - r + r)(8 - r - r) \quad \Rightarrow 8 \times 2r = (8)(8 - 2r)$$
$$\Rightarrow \quad 2r = 8 - 2r \quad \Rightarrow \quad 4r = 8 \Rightarrow \quad r = 2$$

The area of the circles B and C is $2\pi \times (2)^2 = 8\pi$.

The area of the circle A is $\pi \times (4)^2 = 16\pi$.

The fraction of the area that is not shaded is $8\pi + 16\pi = 24\pi$, and hence the fraction of the area that is shaded is $32\pi - 24\pi = 8\pi$.

The answer is $\dfrac{8\pi}{32\pi} = \dfrac{1}{4}$.

24. D.

Extend CB and DA to meet at F. $\triangle CFD$ is then an isosceles triangle and $CF = CD$. Since $CE \perp DF$, CE is the angle bisector of $\angle BCD$, and CE is also the median on DF,

$S_{\triangle CEF} = S_{\triangle CDE}$.

Because $DE = EF$, $DE = 2AE$, so

$EA = AF = \dfrac{1}{4}FD$. $FB = \dfrac{1}{4}FC$.

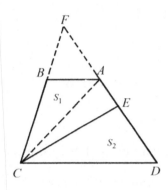

Thus $S_{\triangle FBA} = \dfrac{1}{4}S_{\triangle FAC} = \dfrac{1}{8}S_{\triangle FEC} = \dfrac{1}{8}(S_1 + S_{\triangle FBA})$

$\Rightarrow \quad 8S_{\triangle FBA} = S_1 + S_{\triangle FBA} \quad \Rightarrow$

$7S_{\triangle FBA} = S_1 \quad \Rightarrow \quad S_{\triangle FBA} = \dfrac{28}{7} = 4$.

$S_2 = S_{\triangle FBA} + S_1 = 4 + 28 = 32$.

25. E.

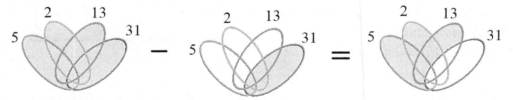

The union of A, B, C, and D can be found by:

$n(A \cup B \cup C \cup D) = n(A) + n(B) + n(C) + n(D)$

$- n(A \cap B) - n(A \cap C) - n(A \cap D) - n(B \cap C) - n(B \cap D) - n(C \cap D)$

$+ n(A \cap B \cap C) + n(A \cap B \cap D) + n(A \cap C \cap D) + n(B \cap C \cap D)$

$- n(A \cap B \cap C \cap D).$

The number of positive integers not exceeding 2015 are multiples of 2, or 5 or 13 or 31 is

$$\left\lfloor \frac{4030}{2} \right\rfloor + \left\lfloor \frac{4030}{5} \right\rfloor + \left\lfloor \frac{4030}{13} \right\rfloor + \left\lfloor \frac{4030}{31} \right\rfloor$$

$$- \left\lfloor \frac{4030}{2\times 5} \right\rfloor - \left\lfloor \frac{4030}{2\times 13} \right\rfloor - \left\lfloor \frac{4030}{2\times 31} \right\rfloor - \left\lfloor \frac{4030}{5\times 13} \right\rfloor - \left\lfloor \frac{4030}{5\times 31} \right\rfloor - \left\lfloor \frac{4030}{13\times 31} \right\rfloor$$

$$+ \left\lfloor \frac{4030}{2\times 5\times 13} \right\rfloor + \left\lfloor \frac{4030}{2\times 5\times 31} \right\rfloor + \left\lfloor \frac{4030}{2\times 13\times 31} \right\rfloor + \left\lfloor \frac{4030}{5\times 13\times 31} \right\rfloor - \left\lfloor \frac{4030}{2\times 5\times 13\times 31} \right\rfloor$$

$$= 2015 + 806 + 310 + 130 - 403 - 155 - 65 - 62 - 26 - 10 + 31 + 13 + 5 + 2 - 1 = 2590.$$

The number of positive integers not exceeding 2015 that are multiples of 9 is

$$\left\lfloor \frac{4030}{31} \right\rfloor = 130$$

The answer is $2590 - 130 = 2460$.

American Mathematics Competitions

Practice 10
AMC 10

(American Mathematics Contest 10)

INSTRUCTIONS

1. This is a twenty-five question multiple choice test. Each question is followed by answers marked A, B, C, D and E. Only one of these is correct.

2. You will have 75 minutes to complete the test.

3. No aids are permitted other than scratch paper, graph paper, rulers, and erasers. No problems on the test will require the use of a calculator.

4. Figures are not necessarily drawn to scale.

5. SCORING: You will receive 6 points for each correct answer, 1.5 points for each problem left unanswered, and 0 points for each incorrect answer.

1. One can holds 15 ounces of soda. What is the minimum number of cans needed to provide three gallons (1 gallon = 128 ounces) of soda?

(A) 27   (B) 26   (C) 25   (D) 20   (E) 18

2. The sums of three whole numbers taken in pairs are 17, 18, and 25. What is the middle number?

(A) 11   (B) 12   (C) 13   (D) 14   (E) 15

3. Simplify as a common fraction: $\dfrac{1}{1+\dfrac{1}{1+\dfrac{2}{3}}}$.

(A) 1/8   (B) 2/8   (C) 3/8   (D) 5/8   (E) 7/8

4. Thirty percent less than 70 is two-fifth more than what number?

(A) 26   (B) 30   (C) 32   (D) 35   (E) 48

5. Kathy has two younger twin brothers. The product of their three ages is 1024. What is the smallest possible sum of their three ages?

(A) 32   (B) 24   (C) 22   (D) 18   (E) 16

6. In a class of 42 students, 18 students are in the Math Club, 5 students are in both the Math Club and the Science Club, and 14 are in neither. How many students are in the Science Club?

(A) 5   (B) 15   (C) 20   (D) 35   (E) 30

7. The number of centimeters in the length, width and height of a rectangular carton are consecutive integers. Find the smallest 4-digit number that could represent the number of cubic centimeters in the volume)

(A) 1001   (B) 1320   (C) 1331   (D) 1025   (E) 1216

8. A majority of the 40 students in Ms. Li's class bought pencils at the school bookstore. Each of these students bought the same number of pencils, and this number was greater than 1. The cost of a pencil in cents was greater than the number of pencils each student bought, and the total cost of all the pencils was $20.15. How many students in the class bought the pencils?

(A) 35   (B) 11   (C) 33   (D) 13   (E) 31

9. Which of the following is equal to Simplify $\sqrt{6-\sqrt{11}} + \sqrt{6+\sqrt{11}}$.
(A) $\sqrt{22}$ (B) 12   (C) $12+\sqrt{22}$ (D) $6+\sqrt{22}$ (E) $2\sqrt{3}$

10. As shown below, convex pentagon $ABCDE$ has sides $AB = 3$, $BC = 4$, $CD = 6$, $DE = 2$, and $EA = 7$. The pentagon is originally positioned in the plane with vertex A at the origin and vertex B on the positive x-axis. The pentagon is then rolled clockwise to the right along the x-axis. Which side will touch the point $x = 2015$ and be completely on the x-axis?
(A) AB (B) BC (C) CD (D) DE (E) EA

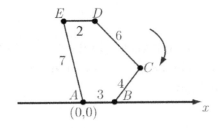

11. *ABCD* is a parallelogram. All the line segments inside the figure either parallel to *AD*, *AD*, or *BE*. How many parallelograms are there that contain the shaded triangle?

(A) 6   (B) 7   (C) 8   (D) 9   (E) 12

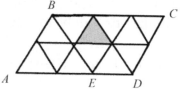

12. A 5 × 5 × 5 wooden cube is painted on five of its faces and is then cut into 125 unit cubes. One unit cube is randomly selected and rolled. What is the probability that the face showing is painted? Express your answer as a fraction.

(A) $\dfrac{1}{6}$ (B) $\dfrac{1}{3}$ (C) $\dfrac{1}{5}$ (D) $\dfrac{2}{7}$ (E) $\dfrac{28}{125}$

13. The lengths of the parallel bases of a trapezoid are 14 cm and 7 cm. One of the legs has length 8 cm. How many integer values are possible for the length of the other leg?

(A) 6   (B) 7   (C) 8   (D) 9   (E) 13

14. It takes Amy 4 hours to paint a house, it takes Bill 6 hours, and it takes Chandra 8 hours. Amy starts to paint the house for one hour, then Bill continues the job for another hour, and Chandra follows Bill and works for one hour. If the pattern continues until the job is completed, how many hours does Chandra paint the house?

(A) $\dfrac{4}{3}$ (B) $\dfrac{1}{3}$ (C) $\dfrac{5}{3}$ (D) 2   (E) $\dfrac{2}{3}$

15. Alex can jog 120 meters in 1 minute, Bob can jog 80 meters in 1 minute, and Charlie can jog 70 meters in 1 minute. The circular path has a circumference of 1000 meters. They start running together at 10:00 a.m. at point A. At what time will they first all be together again at point A?

(A) 10: 40 a.m.   (B) 10:50 a.m.   (C) 11:20 a.m.   (D) 11:40 a.m.   (E) 11:55 a.m.

16. We are choosing a committee of 6 animals from 3 cats, 4 dogs, and 5 pigs. If Alex Cat, Bob Dog and Charles Pig do not like each other and they will not work in the same group, how many compatible committees are there?

(A) 84   (B) 220   (C) 304   (D) 378   (E) 462

17. What is the remainder when $3^1 + 3^2 + \cdots + 3^{2015}$ is divided by 8?

(A) 7   (B) 6   (C) 5   (D) 4   (E) 3

18. The capacity of a car's radiator is nine liters. The mixture of antifreeze and water is 40% antifreeze. The temperature is predicted to drop rapidly requiring the mixture to be 70% antifreeze. How much of the mixture in the radiator must be drawn off and replaced with pure antifreeze?

A. 3.5 liters   B. 4.5 liters   C. 5.0 liters   D. 6.0 liters   E. none of these

19. The sum of a four-digit positive integer and its digits is exactly 2015. Find the sum of all possible values of the four-digit positive integer.

(A) 2015   (B) 2012   (C) 4004   (D) 4008   (E) 4030

20. Pipe A will fill a tank in 6 hours. Pipe B will fill the same tank in 4 hours. Pipe C will fill the tank in the same number of hours that it will take Pipes A and B working together to fill the tank. Three pipes work together for one hour and Pipe C quits working. How many more hours does it take for pipes A and B to finish the job?

(A) $\dfrac{4}{3}$ (B) $\dfrac{5}{3}$ (C) $\dfrac{2}{5}$ (D) $\dfrac{3}{5}$ (E) $\dfrac{2}{3}$

21. In $\triangle ABC$ points D and E lie on BC and AC, respectively. If AD and BE intersect at T so that $AT/DT = 5$ and $BT/ET = 7$, what is CD /BD?

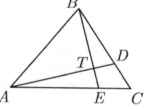

(A) $\dfrac{3}{17}$ (B) $\dfrac{5}{7}$ (C) $\dfrac{4}{17}$ (D) $\dfrac{4}{7}$ (E) $\dfrac{1}{7}$

22. The area of right triangle ABC is 360. $\angle BAC = 90°$. AD is the median on BC. $DE \perp AB$. AD an CE meet at F. Find the area of triangle AEF.

(A) 60   (B) 70   (C) 80   (D) 90   (E) 100

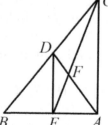

23. *P* is a point inside the equilateral triangle *ABC*. *PA* = 2, *PB* = $2\sqrt{3}$, and *PC* = 4. Find the area of triangle *ABC*.

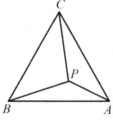

(A) $7\sqrt{3}$ (B) $4\sqrt{3}$ (C) $7\sqrt{38}$ (D) $8\sqrt{38}$

(E) $7\sqrt{2}$

24. A special deck of cards contains cards numbered 1 through 5 for each of five suits. Each of the 25 cards has a club, diamond, heart or spade on one side and the number 1, 2, 3, 4 or 5 on the other side. After a dealer mixed up the cards, three were selected at random. What is the probability that of these three randomly selected cards, displayed here, one of the cards showing the number 3 has a spade printed on the other side? Express your answer as a common fraction.

(A) $\dfrac{4}{11}$ (B) $\dfrac{4}{9}$ (C) $\dfrac{25}{54}$ (D) $\dfrac{5}{11}$ (E) $\dfrac{5}{9}$

25. Circles *A*, *B*, and *C* are externally tangent to each other and internally tangent to circle *D*. Circles *B* and *C* are congruent with radius 8. Circle *A* passes through the center of *D*. What is the radius of circle *A*?

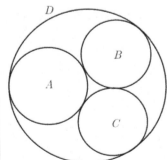

(A) 6   (B) 7   (C) 8   (D) 9   (E) 10

ANSWER KEYS

1. B.
2. B.
3. D.
4. D.
5. A.
6. B.
7. B.
8. E.
9. A.
10. C.
11. E.
12. A.
13. E.
14. A.
15. D.
16. E.
17. A.
18. B.
19. C.
20. C.
21. A.
22. A.
23. A.
24. B.
25. D.

SOLUTIONS:

1. B.
Because $3 \times 128 / 13 = 25.6$, there must be 26 cans.

2. B.
Let three numbers be a, b, and c.

$a + b = 17$	(1)
$b + c = 25$	(2)
$c + a = 18$	(3)
$(1) + (2) + (3)$: $2(a + b + c) = 60$ $\Rightarrow$ $a + b + c = 30$	(4)

$(4) - (3)$: $b = 12$.

3. D.
$$\cfrac{1}{1+\cfrac{1}{1+\cfrac{2}{3}}} = \cfrac{1}{1+\cfrac{1}{\frac{5}{3}}} = \cfrac{1}{1+\frac{3}{5}} = \cfrac{1}{\frac{8}{5}} = \frac{5}{8}.$$

4. D.
Thirty percent less than 70 is $70 - \dfrac{30}{100} \times 70 = \dfrac{2}{5}x + x \qquad \Rightarrow \dfrac{7}{5}x = 49$

$\Rightarrow x = 35$

5. A.
The age of each person is a factor of $1024 = 2^{10}$. Since we want the smallest sum, the three numbers should be as close as possible.

$2^{10} = 2^3 \times 2^3 \times 2^4$.
The twins could be 8, and 8. Kathy could 16.
The smallest sum of their ages is $8 + 8 + 16 = 32$.

6. B.

There are $42 - 14 = 28$ students participated in the two clubs. Let S be the number of students in the Science Club.

By the Two Events Union Formula $n(A \cup B) = n(A) + n(B) - n(A \cap B)$, we have $28 = 18 + S - 5$. So $S = 15$.

7. B.

Let the smallest value of the length, width and height be $a - 1$. Since the numbers are consecutive integers, then the other two dimensions are a and $a + 1$.

$V = (a - 1) \times a \times (a + 1) = a^3 - a$

We are seeking for a 4-digit number (a^3) that is just over 1000.

$10^3 = 1000$ and $11^3 = 1331$.

So $a = 11$. $V = a^3 - a = 11^3 - 11 = 1320$.

8. E.

Let C be the cost of a pencil in cents, N be the number of pencils each student bought, and S be the number of students who bought pencils. Then $C \cdot N \cdot S = 2015 = 5 \cdot 13 \cdot 31$, and $C > N > 1$. Because a majority of the students bought pencils, $40 \geq S > 40/2 = 20$. Therefore $S = 31$, $N = 5$, and $C = 13$.

9. A.

Method 1:

Let $\sqrt{6 - \sqrt{11}} + \sqrt{6 + \sqrt{11}} = x$ (1)

Squaring both sides of (1): $(\sqrt{6 - \sqrt{11}} + \sqrt{6 + \sqrt{11}})^2 = x^2 \Rightarrow$

$(\sqrt{6 - \sqrt{11}} + \sqrt{6 + \sqrt{11}})^2 = 6 - \sqrt{11} + 2\sqrt{(6 - \sqrt{11})(6 + \sqrt{11})} + 6 + \sqrt{11}$

$= 12 + 2\sqrt{(6 - \sqrt{11})(6 + \sqrt{11})} = 12 + 2\sqrt{6^2 - 11} = 12 + 2\sqrt{25} = 12 + 10 = 22$.

$x^2 = 22 \qquad \Rightarrow \qquad x = \sqrt{22}$.

Method 2:

We see that $a = 6$, $b = 11$, and $a^2 - b = 6^2 - 11 = 25 = 5^2$. Therefore the given nested radical can be denested.

By the formula, we have

$$\sqrt{6+\sqrt{11}} = \sqrt{\frac{6+\sqrt{6^2-11}}{2}} + \sqrt{\frac{6-\sqrt{6^2-11}}{2}} = \sqrt{\frac{11}{2}} + \sqrt{\frac{1}{2}}.$$

Similarly, $\sqrt{6-\sqrt{11}} = \sqrt{\frac{6+\sqrt{6^2-11}}{2}} - \sqrt{\frac{6-\sqrt{6^2-11}}{2}} = \sqrt{\frac{11}{2}} - \sqrt{\frac{1}{2}}.$

Thus $\sqrt{6-\sqrt{11}} + \sqrt{6+\sqrt{11}} = \sqrt{\frac{11}{2}} + \sqrt{\frac{1}{2}} + \sqrt{\frac{11}{2}} - \sqrt{\frac{1}{2}} = 2\sqrt{\frac{11}{2}} = 2\sqrt{\frac{2\times11}{2\times2}} = \sqrt{22}.$

10. C.
One complete rotation goes $3 + 4 + 6 + 2 + 7 = 22$ unit length.
$2015 = 22 \times 91 + 13$.
We only need to roll the pentagon 13 units. $3 + 4 + 6 = 13$. Therefore CD will touch $x = 2015$ and be completely on the x-axis.

11. E.
We have $\begin{pmatrix} 2 \\ 1 \end{pmatrix} \times \begin{pmatrix} 2 \\ 1 \end{pmatrix} \times \begin{pmatrix} 2 \\ 1 \end{pmatrix} \times \begin{pmatrix} 1 \\ 1 \end{pmatrix} = 8$

Parallelograms with sides parallel to AB and BC.

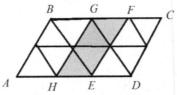

We have $\begin{pmatrix} 1 \\ 1 \end{pmatrix} \times \begin{pmatrix} 2 \\ 1 \end{pmatrix} \times \begin{pmatrix} 2 \\ 1 \end{pmatrix} \times \begin{pmatrix} 1 \\ 1 \end{pmatrix} = 4$ more parallelograms with sides parallel to BE

and BC.
Total number of parallelograms that contain the shaded triangle is 12.

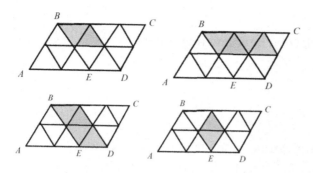

12. A.

Method 1:

There are $5 \cdot 25 = 125$ painted faces all of which are equally likely. There are 125 $\cdot$ 6 = 750 faces altogether. Therefore the probability is 125/750 = 1/6.

Method 2:

Number of cubes painted 1 face: $12 \times 4 + 9 = 57$.
Number of cubes painted 2 faces: $12 \times 2 + 4 = 28$.
Number of cubes painted 3 faces: 4.
Number of cubes painted 0 side: 27 (We do not need this information).

The probability is $P = \dfrac{57}{125} \times \dfrac{1}{6} + \dfrac{28}{125} \times \dfrac{2}{6} + \dfrac{4}{125} \times \dfrac{3}{6} = \dfrac{1}{6}$.

13. E.

$\dfrac{a}{7} = \dfrac{a+8}{14} = \dfrac{8}{7} \Rightarrow \qquad a = 8$.

$\dfrac{a}{b} = \dfrac{8}{x} \Rightarrow \qquad b = x$.

By the triangle inequality theorem,

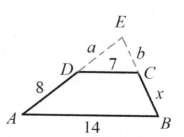

$AE - AB < EB < AE + AB \quad \Rightarrow$
$\qquad 16 - 14 < x + x < 16 + 14 \Rightarrow \quad 2 < 2x < 30$
$\Rightarrow 1 < x < 15 \quad \Rightarrow \qquad 2 \le x \le 14$.

The number of integer values for the length of the other leg is then $14 - 2 + 1 = 13$.

14. A.

In the first 3 hours, each person works one hour and they finish

$(\frac{1}{4}+\frac{1}{6}+\frac{1}{8})\times 1 = \frac{13}{24}$ of the job.

The job left is $\frac{11}{24}$.

Let x be the number of hours Chandra works. In the next round, we have

$$\frac{1}{4}\times 1 + \frac{1}{6}\times 1 + \frac{1}{8}\times x = \frac{11}{24} \qquad \Rightarrow \qquad \frac{1}{8}\times x = \frac{11}{24} - \frac{1}{4} - \frac{1}{6} = \frac{11-6-4}{24} = \frac{1}{24} \Rightarrow$$

$$x = \frac{1}{3}$$

So Chandra paints the house $1 + \frac{1}{3} = \frac{4}{3}$ hours.

15. D.

Method 1:

We find the time needed for each person to complete the path.

Alex needs $\frac{1000}{120} = \frac{25}{3}$ minutes.

Bob needs $\frac{1000}{80} = \frac{25}{2}$ minutes.

Charlie needs $\frac{1000}{70} = \frac{100}{7}$ minutes.

We now find the least common multiple of them.

$$LCM(\frac{a}{b},\frac{c}{d}) = \frac{ac}{GCF(ad,bc)} = \frac{LCM(ad,bc)}{bd}$$

$$LCM(\frac{25}{3},\frac{25}{2}) = \frac{25\times 25}{GCF(25\times 2, 25\times 3)} = \frac{25\times 25}{25} = 25$$

$$LCM(25,\frac{100}{7}) = LCM(\frac{25}{1},\frac{100}{7}) = \frac{25\times 100}{GCF(25\times 7, 100\times 1)} = \frac{25\times 100}{25} = 100.$$

So at 11:40 a.m. they will first all be together again at point A.

Method 2:

Time needed for Alex to catch Bob is $1000 \div (120 - 80) = 25$ minutes

Time needed for Alex to catch Charlie is $1000 \div (120 - 70) = 20$ minutes

Time needed for Bob to catch Charlie is $1000 \div (80 - 70) = 100$ minutes

$LCM\,(25, 20, 10) = 100$.

So at 11:40 a.m. they will first all be together again at point A.

16. E.

A compatible group will either exclude all these three animals or include exactly one of them. This can be done in $\binom{9}{6} + \binom{3}{1}\binom{9}{5} = 84 + 378 = 462$ committees.

17. A.

The remainder is 1 when 3^n is divided by 8, where n is even. So the sum of every 8 terms will have a remainder of 0 when divided by 8.

$2014/2 = 1007 = 121 \times 8 + 7$. So the remainder is 7 when $3^2 + 3^4 + \cdots + 3^{2014}$ is divided by 8.

The remainder is 3 when 3^m is divided by 8, where m is odd. So the sum of every 8 terms will have a remainder of 0 when divided by 8.

$(2015 - 1)/2 + 1 = 1008 = 126 \times 8 + 0$. So the remainder is 0 when $3^1 + 3^3 + \cdots + 3^{2015}$ is divided by 8.

So the required remainder is $7 + 0 = 7$.

18. B.

Let x be the amount of antifreeze to be drained off.

Name	C	V	S
A_1	0.4	9	3.6
	0.4	x	$0.4\,x$
A_2	0.4	$9 - x$	$0.4(9 - x)$

B	1.0	x	$1.0\,x$
Mixture	0.7	9	0.7(9)

$$0.4(9 - x) + 1.0\,x = 0.7(9) \quad \Rightarrow \quad x = 4.5 \text{ liters.}$$

19. C.

The four-digit positive integer can be written as $1000a + 100b + 10c + d$, where a, b, c, and d are digits.

We have $1000a + 100b + 10c + d + a + b + c + d = 2015 \quad \Rightarrow$

$1001a + 101b + 11c + 2d = 2015$.

Case 1: $a = 2$.

$1001a + 101b + 11c + 2d = 2015 \quad \Rightarrow \quad 101b + 11c + 2d = 2015 - 2002 = 13$.

So $b = 0$, $c = 1$, and $d = 1$.

The four-digit positive integer is 2011.

Case 2: $a = 1$.

$1001a + 101b + 11c + 2d = 2015 \quad \Rightarrow \quad 101b + 11c + 2d = 2015 - 1001 = 1014$.

So $b = 9$, $c = 9$, and $2d = 1014 - 909 - 99 = (105 - 99) = 6$. So $d = 3$.

The four-digit positive integer is 1993.

The answer is $2011 + 1993 = 4004$.

20. C.

Pipe A works at a rate of $\dfrac{1}{6}$ (tank/hour) and Pipe B works at a rate of $\dfrac{1}{4}$. Working together, they fill the tank at a rate of $(\dfrac{1}{6} + \dfrac{1}{4}) = \dfrac{5}{12}$. So Pipe C works at the rate of $\dfrac{5}{12}$.

Three pipes work together for one hour, the job is done: $(\dfrac{1}{6} + \dfrac{1}{4} + \dfrac{5}{12}) \times 1 = \dfrac{5}{6}$.

Let t be the time needed for A and B to finish the rest of the job working together.

We have $(\dfrac{1}{6}+\dfrac{1}{4})t = \dfrac{1}{6}$ $\qquad \Rightarrow \qquad t = \dfrac{2}{5}$.

21. A.

Method 1:

Draw $DF \parallel BE$.

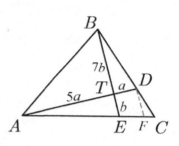

$\triangle ADF \sim \triangle ATE.$ $\dfrac{AD}{AT} = \dfrac{DF}{TE} \Rightarrow \dfrac{6a}{5a} = \dfrac{DF}{b} \Rightarrow DF = \dfrac{6b}{5}$

$\triangle CBE \sim \triangle CDF.$ $\dfrac{BE}{DF} = \dfrac{BC}{CD} \Rightarrow \dfrac{8b}{DF} = \dfrac{BC}{CD}$

$\Rightarrow \qquad \dfrac{8b}{\dfrac{6b}{5}} = \dfrac{BC}{CD} \qquad \Rightarrow \qquad \dfrac{20}{3} = \dfrac{BC}{CD}$

$\Rightarrow \qquad \dfrac{20}{3} = \dfrac{BD+CD}{CD} \Rightarrow \dfrac{20}{3} = \dfrac{BD}{CD}+1$

$\Rightarrow \qquad \dfrac{20}{3}-1 = \dfrac{BD}{CD} = \dfrac{17}{3} \Rightarrow \dfrac{CD}{BD} = \dfrac{3}{17}$.

Method 2:

Draw $EF \parallel AD$.

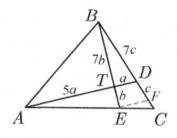

$\triangle BEF \sim \triangle BTD.$ $\dfrac{BE}{BT} = \dfrac{EF}{TD} \Rightarrow \dfrac{8b}{7b} = \dfrac{EF}{a} \Rightarrow EF = \dfrac{8a}{7}$

$\triangle ACD \sim \triangle EFC.$ $\dfrac{AD}{EF} = \dfrac{CD}{CF} \Rightarrow \dfrac{6a}{\dfrac{8a}{7}} = \dfrac{CD}{CF}$

$\Rightarrow \qquad \dfrac{CF}{CD} = \dfrac{4}{21} \qquad \Rightarrow \qquad \dfrac{4}{21} = \dfrac{CD-DF}{CD} = 1-\dfrac{DF}{CD}$

$\Rightarrow \qquad 1-\dfrac{4}{21} = \dfrac{DF}{CD} = \dfrac{17}{21} \Rightarrow CD = \dfrac{21}{17}DF$

$$\frac{CD}{BD} = \frac{\frac{21}{17}DF}{7DF} = \frac{3}{17}.$$

Method 3:
Draw $DF /\!/ AC$.

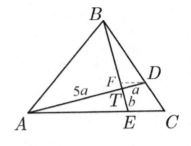

$\triangle AET \sim \triangle DFT$. $\dfrac{AT}{DT} = \dfrac{TE}{TF} \Rightarrow \dfrac{5a}{a} = \dfrac{b}{TF} \Rightarrow \quad TF = \dfrac{b}{5}$

$\triangle BEC \sim \triangle BFD$. $\dfrac{BE}{BF} = \dfrac{BC}{BD} \Rightarrow \qquad \dfrac{8b}{BT - TF} = \dfrac{BC}{BD}$

$\Rightarrow \qquad \dfrac{8b}{7b - \dfrac{b}{5}} = \dfrac{BC}{BD} \Rightarrow \qquad \dfrac{8b}{\dfrac{34}{5}b} = \dfrac{BD - CD}{BD}$

$\Rightarrow \qquad \dfrac{20}{17} = 1 - \dfrac{CD}{BD} \Rightarrow \qquad \dfrac{CD}{BD} = \dfrac{20}{17} - 1 = \dfrac{3}{17}$

22. A.

Method 1:
Draw $FG \perp AB$.
$FG /\!/ DE /\!/ AC$.

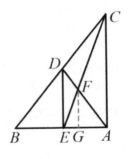

$$\frac{1}{DE} + \frac{1}{AC} = \frac{1}{FG} \qquad \Rightarrow \qquad \frac{1}{\frac{1}{2}AC} + \frac{1}{AC} = \frac{1}{FG}$$

$$\Rightarrow \qquad \frac{3}{AC} = \frac{1}{FG} \Rightarrow \qquad FG = \frac{AC}{3}.$$

The area of triangle AEF is $\dfrac{1}{2}AE \times FG = \dfrac{1}{2} \times \dfrac{1}{2}AB \times \dfrac{AC}{3} = \dfrac{1}{6} \times (\dfrac{1}{2}AB \times AC)$

$$= \frac{1}{6}S_{\triangle ABC} = \frac{1}{6} \times 360 = 60$$

Method 2:
Draw $FG \perp AB$.
$FG /\!/ DE /\!/ AC$.

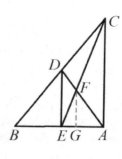

$$\frac{FG}{\frac{1}{2}AC} = \frac{FG}{DE} = \frac{AG}{AE} \qquad (1)$$

$$\frac{FG}{AC} = \frac{EG}{AE} \qquad (2)$$

$$(1)+(2): \frac{3FG}{AC} = \frac{AE}{AE} = 1 \quad \Rightarrow \quad FG = \frac{AC}{3}.$$

The area of triangle AEF is

$$\frac{1}{2}AE \times FG = \frac{1}{2} \times \frac{1}{2}AB \times \frac{AC}{3} = \frac{1}{6} \times (\frac{1}{2}AB \times AC) = \frac{1}{6}S_{\triangle ABC} = \frac{1}{6} \times 360 = 60.$$

23. A.

We rotate $\triangle BAP$ anti clock wise $60°$ such that BA and BC overlap. PB will be in the position of BM, and PA will be in the position of MC. So $BM = BP$, $MC = PA$, $\angle PBM = 60°$.

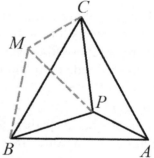

Thus $\triangle BPM$ is an equilateral triangle.

Therefore $PM = PB = 2\sqrt{3}$.

In $\triangle MCP$, $PC = 4$. $MC = PA = 2$, $PM = 2\sqrt{3}$. We see that $PC^2 = PM^2 + MC^2$, and $PC = 2MC$.

So $\triangle MCP$ is a right triangle with $\angle CMP = 90°$ and $\angle CPM = 30°$.

We also know that $\triangle PBM$ is an equilateral triangle with $\angle BPM = 60°$. Then we know that $\triangle BPC$ is a right triangle with $\angle BPC = 90°$.

Thus $BC^2 = BP^2 + PC^2 = (2\sqrt{3})^2 + 4^2 = 28 \Rightarrow BC = 2\sqrt{7}$.

The area of triangle ABC is $\frac{BC^2}{4}\sqrt{3} = \frac{(2\sqrt{7})^2}{4}\sqrt{3} = 7\sqrt{3}$.

24. B.
Case 1: The middle card, showing the spade, does not have a 3 printed on the other side.

There are four possible ways for the back of the middle card: 1, 2, 4, or 5. There are 4 possible ways for the back of the left side card: 3/club, 3/diamond, 3/heart or 3/spade. There are 3 possible ways for the back of the right side card since one is already taken by the left side card.

There are $4 \times 4 \times 3 = 48$ different ways for this scenario to occur.

Among them, there are $1 \times 4 \times 3 = 12$ ways such that the left side card has the spade on the back, and $3 \times 4 \times 1 = 12$ ways such that the right side card has the spade on the back. That is, we have 24 ways that one of the cards showing the number 3 has a spade printed on the other side.

Case 2: The middle card, showing the spade, has a 3 printed on the other side.

There is only one way for the back of the middle card: 3/spade. There are 3 possible ways for the back of the left side card: 3/club, 3/diamond, or 3/heart. There are 2 possible ways for the back of the right side card since two are taken by the left side card and the middle card.

There are $3 \times 1 \times 2 = 6$ different ways for this scenario to occur. But none of these scenarios has a spade printed on the other side of one of the cards showing the number 3. So of the $48 + 6 = 54$ possible scenarios, the probability that one of the cards showing the number 3 has a spade printed on the other side is $24/54 = 4/9$.

25. D.
Let E, H, and F be the centers of circles A, B, and D, respectively, and let G be the point of tangency of circles B and C.
Connect EH, EC, CH, and EG.
Since circles B and C are congruent, we know that EG is the perpendicular bisector of HC.

Let $x = EF$ and $y = FG$.

Since the center of circle D lies on circle A and the circles have a common point of tangency, the radius of circle D is $2x$, which is the diameter of circle A.

Draw the line l tangent to circles D and B at K. Connect KF and we know that KF goes through H.

Applying the Pythagorean Theorem to right triangles EGH and FGH gives:

$$(x+8)^2 - (x+y)^2 = 8^2 \qquad (1)$$
$$(2x-8)^2 - y^2 = 8^2 \qquad (2)$$

(1) can be simplified to $y^2 + 2xy - 16x = 0$ (3)

(2) can be simplified to $4x^2 - 32x - y^2 = 0$ (4)

(3) + (4): $4x^2 - 48x + 2xy = 0 \qquad \Rightarrow \qquad 2x^2 - 24x + xy = 0 \qquad \Rightarrow$

$\qquad x(2x - 24 + y) = 0$.

We know tha $x \neq 0$. So we have $2x - 24 + y = 0 \qquad \Rightarrow \qquad y = 24 - 2x$ (5)

Subsituting (5) into (4): $4x^2 - 32x - (24 - 2x)^2 = 0$

$\Rightarrow \qquad 4x^2 - 32x - 24^2 - 4x^2 + 2 \times 2 \times 24x = 0 \qquad \Rightarrow \qquad 64x - 24^2 = 0 \Rightarrow$

$\qquad x = 9$.

Made in the
USA
Middletown, DE